Émilie Penou

21 DAYS TO LEARN TO crochet amigurumi

× *daily practice* ×

× *step-by-step instructions* ×

× *7 projects* ×

21 Days to Learn to Crochet Amigurumi

First published in the United States in 2026 by Stash Books, an imprint of C&T Publishing, Inc., P.O. Box 1456, Lafayette, CA 94549

This edition of "*21 jours pour apprendre à crocheter des amigurumis*" first published in France by Éditions Marie Claire in 2024 is published by arrangement with Marie Claire.

PUBLISHER: Amy Barrett-Daffin

CREATIVE DIRECTOR: Gailen Runge

SENIOR EDITOR: Roxane Cerda

ENGLISH LANGUAGE COVER DESIGNER AND LAYOUT ARTIST: April Mostek

ENGLISH TRANSLATION: Kristy Darling Finder

PRODUCTION COORDINATORS: Casey Dukes and Zinnia Heinzmann

EDITING: Julie Bez

CREATION, PRODUCTION, EXPLANATIONS: Émilie Penou

REVISION: Véronique Blanc

PHOTOGRAPHY: Pierre Nicou

GRAPHIC DESIGN: Émilie Laudrin

LAYOUT: Littopia

COVER DESIGN: Claire Morel Fatio

ISBN: 978-1-64403-627-3

Printed in China

10 9 8 7 6 5 4 3 2 1

to LEARN TO CROCHET AMIGURUMI

INTRODUCTION
AND ADVICE

Hi!

We are going to spend 21 days together to learn how to crochet amigurumi. This book is for everyone, whether or not you have prior experience with crochet. Naturally, the first four days will be easier for those who already know the stitches, but revisiting the basics is always helpful—for remembering what the stitches are called, discovering new techniques, practicing, or just having fun checking your skills.

The level of the lessons will increase gradually. You will begin with the basic crochet stitches before learning more complex ones. Of course, you won't encounter every crochet stitch, but I've spotlighted those most frequently used for amigurumi so you can focus on them.

You will have the same number of days for learning as for creating your amigurumi. In my opinion, there's nothing better than putting your lessons into practice in order to truly understand them, and I hope you'll like the little Woods Family, because they can't wait to come to life at the tip of your crochet hook.

I recommend taking your time. Complete one day, then practice making rows until the motions feel natural. And above all, don't undo your work! We're not looking for perfection from the outset, because that does nothing but create frustration. Are there holes? It's okay. Are there too many or too few stitches? It's okay. Continue your rows, see what's not working, and return to the lesson photos. If your work becomes impossible to work, cut the yarn and start over. In the beginning this can be discouraging, but when you're done, you'll have all your work in front of you and you'll feel so accomplished.

Because I am right-handed, the step-by-step photos in this book show the left hand holding the yarn and the right hand holding the hook. If you are left-handed, don't try to crochet with your right hand, but use your left hand as you would to write. Because the hook is usually held like a pencil, this will be more logical for you and it's not worth working against your brain. You will crochet from left to right, whereas the photos show the steps from right to left, so focus the explanation and the movement of the yarn above all else. The most important thing is to discover the movement that feels best to you, whether you're right- or left-handed. Once you have the logic, the next 21 days will be a breeze.

One last piece of advice: This book is laid out in 21 days, but if you need several days to get something down, that's not a problem. Don't put pressure on yourself. The goal is, when you close the book, to look at what you've made and be proud of yourself, whether it took 21 days or twice as long. Go at your own pace, take a break if you get frustrated, but always try to make at least two rows a day, as muscle memory is very important in crochet and requires that you work often, even if just a little.

Émilie

GLOSSARY
AND ABBREVIATIONS

rnd (round)

Rounds are crocheted in a spiral (using a magic ring is recommended).

r (row)

Rows are crocheted to the end and back again.

ch (chain stitch)

Tie a loop on your hook, yarn over (take some yarn) then draw a loop through the stitch. Yarn over again and draw a loop through the stitch. Repeat as many times as necessary to get the right number of stitches (see Day 2).

Magic ring

See Day 3.

sc (single crochet)

Insert the hook through the stitch in previous row, yarn over (take some yarn) then draw a loop through the stitch. Yarn over again and draw it through both loops on the hook (see Day 2).

sl st (slip stitch)

Insert the hook through the stitch in the previous row, yarn over (take some yarn) then draw a loop through both loops on your hook (see Day 4).

hdc (half double crochet)

Yarn over, insert the hook into the stitch in the previous row, yarn over then draw a loop through the stitch. You now have three loops on your hook, yarn over again and pull through all three loops (see Day 10).

lp st (loop stitch)

See Day 16.

bo (bobble)

See Day 19.

p (picot)

Chain three then make a slip stitch behind the first chain (in the back "bump"). See Day 6.

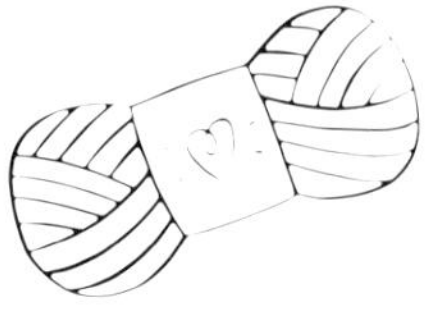

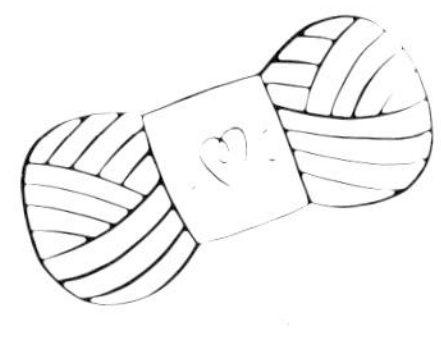

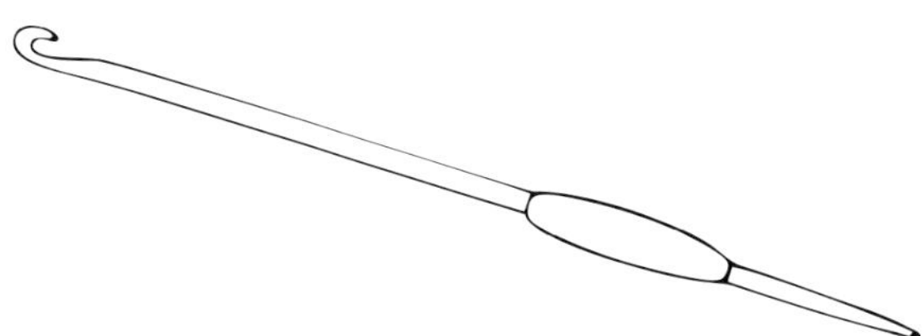

inc (increase)

Crochet 2 sc in the same stitch (see Day 2).

inc3 (multiple increase)

Crochet 3 sc in the same stitch (see Day 4).

inc-lp (loop stitch increase)

See Day 16.

dec (simple decrease) / sc2tog (single crochet 2 together)

Insert the hook into the first stitch, yarn over (take some yarn) then draw a loop through the stitch. Insert the hook into the second stitch, yarn over (take some yarn) then draw a loop through the stitch. Yarn over again and draw the yarn through both loops on the hook (see Day 2).

inv dec (invisible decrease)

Insert the hook into the front loop of the first stitch then, without yarning over, insert it into the front loop of the second stitch. Once both loops are on the hook, yarn over and draw the yarn through the two loops. Yarn over again and draw the yarn though both loops (see Day 13).

dec-lp (loop stitch decrease)

See Day 16.

***...*×**

Repeat the instructions between * * the number of times indicated by the ×.

{...}

The instructions between { } are done in the same stitch.

[FL] (front loop) / [BL] (back loop)

Indicates in which loop to crochet the row (see Day 5).

I discover THE MATERIALS

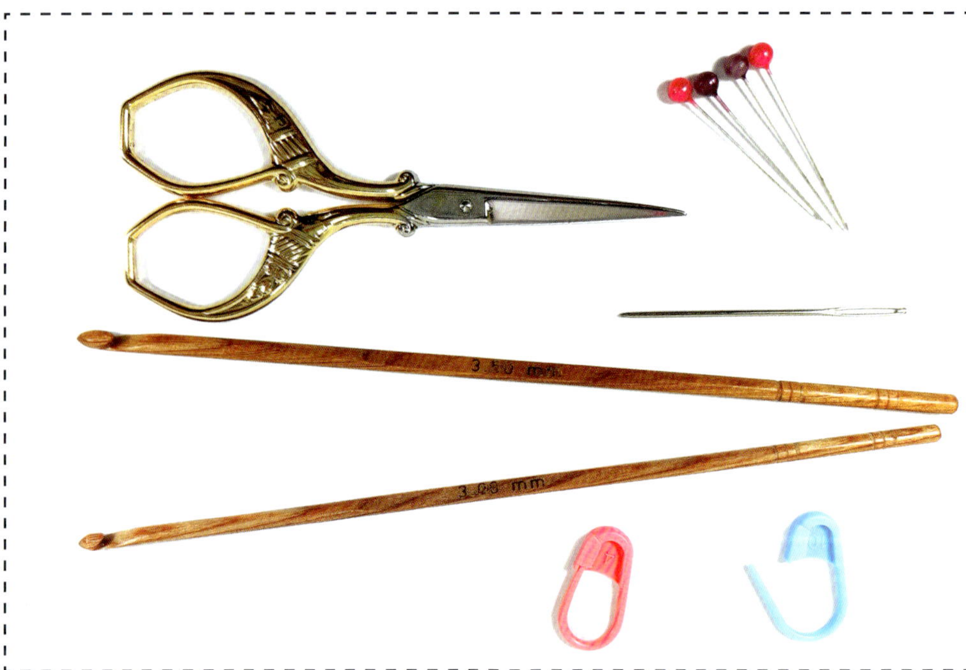

Today's motto: Have fun. You will need specific materials but there's nothing wrong with finding a pretty little pouch or box to put everything in. Crochet doesn't require a lot of space, but there are a lot of small pieces so it's nice to have your materials in a favorite bag for a moment of relaxation.

You will need **one crochet hook size D-3** (3.00mm) **and another size E-4** (3.50mm). Why two sizes? Because you're going to test to see if you crochet loosely or tightly. Until you've completed the first days, you won't be able to answer this question, so it's better to be prepared. The size of the hook is usually marked on it, but if not, you can find gauges in craft shops to determine the size. Then you will need **yarn appropriate to your hook size**. I recommend a Super Fine or Fine yarn when working on your amigurumi projects, such as a fingering, baby, or sport yarn. Look on the label and pick one designed for a 3mm crochet hook.

You can see this is a yarn worked with a size D-3 crochet hook (3.00mm). (If the hook size is not indicated on the label, you can rely on the size recommended for knitting needles.) While the amigurumi in this book are crocheted using the D-3 hook (3.00mm), the lessons will be completed with the E-4 hook (3.50mm) so that you can see your stitches more clearly.

Then you will need **stuffing, scissors for the yarn, stitch markers, yarn needles** (with a blunt end), and pins to help when sewing. You can, of course, add a tape measure to all this, it's always useful.

If you have everything, you can get started!

See you tomorrow for our first stitches!

day 2

Review

SINGLE CROCHET, INCREASES, AND DECREASES

Now that you have taken inventory of your materials and the various tips for crocheting amigurumi (Day 1), we'll review the stitches you'll need for your projects on Days 2–4. Take the time to practice, whether you know the stitches already or not, to achieve a uniformity that will be useful when making your first amigurumi on Day 5. The more instinctive your movements become, the more you'll be able to focus on the pattern. Take your time, take breaks if needed, and never push yourself too hard.

MATERIALS

- E-4 crochet hook (3.50mm)
- Fine/sport weight cotton yarn
- Scissors

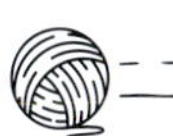

THE CHAIN STITCH

Chaining is the foundation stage of projects that are worked flat or that begin as an oval. Don't worry about your movements or how you hold the yarn at first, just focus on not making your stitches too tight. I also recommend that you don't undo your work so you can see your progress. Your yarn tension is unlikely to be perfect when you start out but it's okay, cut the thread and start over. This will allow you to see your progress and avoid feeling that you're not getting anywhere.

1

Make a slip knot and put it onto your hook. Don't tighten it too much, the loop should be able to slide easily on your hook.

2

Yarn over. This means that you need to wrap the yarn around your hook. So that it's easier to work with, wrap it from the back forward, passing over the hook.

Draw the yarn that you've wrapped around your hook through the loop already on it. This creates your first stitch.

Note: Be sure not to tighten the yarn around your hook and don't forget that your hook is there to help you. Don't hesitate to turn it so that it grabs the yarn well during this delicate step.

Repeat Step 2, yarning over (wrapping the thread around your hook).

Draw the yarn that you've wrapped around your hook through the loop already on it. This creates your second stitch.

Continue until you have 10 stitches.

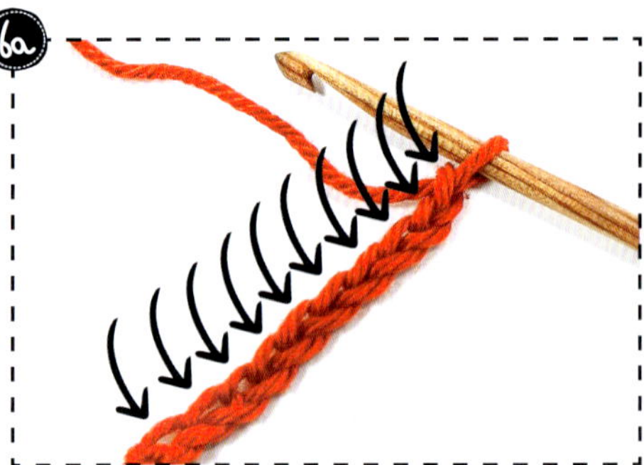

The 10 stitches are made. You can now take a moment to count them. Each "bump" is a stitch, as indicated by the arrows.

Note: The loop on your hook is not counted in the 10 stitches.

Your chain is finished. You can repeat Steps 2–5 as many times as you want until you feel comfortable and until you figure out how to hold your hook and yarn. Don't undo your chains, cut the yarn and make new ones so you can see your progress (after you cut, thread the yarn through the loop on your hook so the chain doesn't come undone).

THE SINGLE CROCHET

The single crochet is crochet's base stitch. Absolutely every amigurumi that you're going to make will be at least 95% made up of single crochets, so you need to master it. As with your chaining, I recommend not undoing your stitches every time you make a mistake, then you can see your progress with each new row, fix your mistakes, see what works and what doesn't with your movements, and there's nothing better than that.

6

First you need to understand where the first stitch goes. The stitch at the base of your hook (indicated by the dot) cannot be worked because your yarn comes out of it, so you can only work in the second stitch (indicated by the arrow) and those beyond it. This will therefore give you 9 stitches and not 10 (because the first is never worked). Don't hesitate to count stitches to figure out where you are.

7

Insert your hook into the second stitch from your hook.

8

Yarn over (wrap the yarn around your hook).

9

Draw the yarn you've wrapped around your hook through the stitch into which you inserted your hook in Step 7.

You now have two loops on your hook.

10

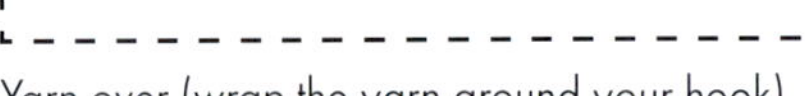

Yarn over (wrap the yarn around your hook).

11

Draw the yarn you've wrapped around your hook through the two loops on your hook.

You have just made your first single crochet (indicated by the dot), the next one will be made where indicated by the arrow.

12

Insert your hook into the next stitch (indicated by the arrow in the previous image) to make the second stitch, repeating Steps 7–11.

13

You have just made your second single crochet (indicated by a second dot), the next one will be made where indicated by the arrow.

Continue repeating these steps for the next 7 stitches (9 total).

14

Here is what you'll have at the end of your first row. You have 9 single crochets (indicated by dots).

Note 1: Be aware that the single crochet on the right is often difficult to see. If it gives you any trouble, don't hesitate to put in a stitch marker so you don't lose it.

Note 2: Take the time to look over your stitches, they are made up of two vertical strands that create a V (shown in green to help you).

15

Before turning your work over to do the second row, you will need to do one chain stitch, just like the stitches you did for the foundation row.

Why do we make a chain stitch at the end of each row? As explained in Step 6b, you can't work in the stitch at the base of your hook. Because of this, you need to compensate for this loss by adding a chain stitch to maintain the correct number of stitches per row.

Yarn over (wrap the yarn around your hook).

16

Draw the yarn you've wrapped around your hook through the loop on the hook. This creates your chain stitch.

You can now turn your work over.

17

This is what gives your work a back. Because you've only done one row, the stitches are hard to see. Therefore I recommend looking at your work from above to get your bearings.

18

Here is the view from above. Your stitches are more visible and are made up of two strands, or loops (indicated in green on one stitch to help you). Unlike the previous row where you inserted your hook through a single loop, you will now need to use both to continue to make your single crochets.

19

Insert your hook into the second stitch from your hook (indicated by the rightmost arrow in the previous image), going under both loops, and repeat Steps 7–11 in the 9 stitches of the previous row to make 9 new stitches.

20

Here is what you have at the end of your second row. All that's left now is to make your chain stitch (see Step 15) and then turn your work to continue your rows.

Starting with the second row, all following rows will be done exactly the same. I recommend making several practice rows following this exercise to figure out your movements and get comfortable. The single crochet needs to become second nature.

INCREASING (SINGLE CROCHET)

An important step in crochet is increasing with the single crochet, which allows you to give shape to your work. There are several ways of increasing, but we will look only at the most commonly used.

21

Repeat the previous steps: Chain 10 stitches then make two rows of single crochets.

Make your chain stitch at the end of row 2 before turning.

22

Increase, first step: Make a single crochet in the first stitch of your row.

Note: The place where you insert your hook to make this first stitch is indicated by a dot and the single crochet by an arrow. Take the time to find these on your own work.

Increase, second step: Insert your hook into the same spot you did in Step 22 (indicated by the dot) and make a new single crochet.

You have your 2 single crochets (indicated by arrows) coming from a single spot (indicated by a dot), so you have just made your first increase.

Continue in this way for the whole row: Make 9 increases in total. The work will deform, that's normal.

Note: The 9 points where you've worked your increases are indicated by dots and one increase is indicated in green so you can visualize it. Just as a single crochet looks like a V (2 vertical strands), an increase looks like a W (4 vertical strands).

DECREASE (SINGLE CROCHET)

Just as important as increasing, decreasing also allows you to give shape to your work. There are several methods of decreasing, but you only need the most commonly used method to start out (other methods will be taught on later days).

You are now going to make a row of decreases.

Insert your hook into the first stitch.

27

Yarn over (wrap the yarn around your hook).

28

Draw the yarn you've wrapped around your hook through the stitch into which you inserted your hook in Step 26.

You now have two loops on your hook.

29

Insert your hook into the next stitch.

30

Yarn over (wrap the yarn around your hook).

31

Draw the yarn you've wrapped around your hook through the stitch into which you inserted your hook in Step 29.

You now have three loops on your hook.

32

Yarn over (wrap the yarn around your hook).

33

Draw the yarn you've wrapped around your hook through the three loops on your hook.

You have just made your first decrease (indicated by an arrow) by making one stitch in two different stitches (indicated by dots). This decrease is also written "single crochet two together" (sc2tog).

34

Continue in this way for the whole row, making 9 decreases. Your work will thus regain its original shape.

Note: Decreases are visible because they are made up of two strands leaning far to the left (indicated twice in green in the photo to help you find them).

You can now work several rows of increases and decreases to get used to making them and also finding them (don't hesitate to look back at the photos for help).

Tomorrow we'll dive into the mysteries of the magic ring.

day 3

I learn about MAGIC RINGS AND STITCH MARKERS

MATERIALS

- E-4 crochet hook (3.50mm)
- Fine/sport weight cotton yarn
- Scissors
- Stitch marker

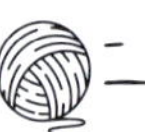

The magic ring can be the most stressful method of starting for beginners, but working step by step, you'll find that you master it perfectly. There is a simple way of doing it and a more complicated way. You are going to do the first (simple) version for the time being, and you can work on the more complicated version after you've learned the basics with your first amigurumi creations. As these are worked in a spiral (meaning you never really stop a row), you will need a stitch marker that opens (different from a knitting stitch marker) to mark where your row begins.

1

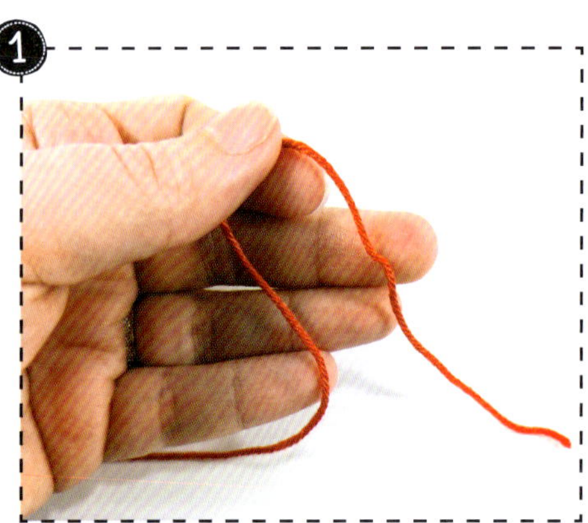

Here is how you hold the yarn. The end is on your right and the rest of the ball is on your left.

2a

Wrap the yarn around your fingers from left to right. Hold the yarn between your fingers to have the right tension.

day 3

2

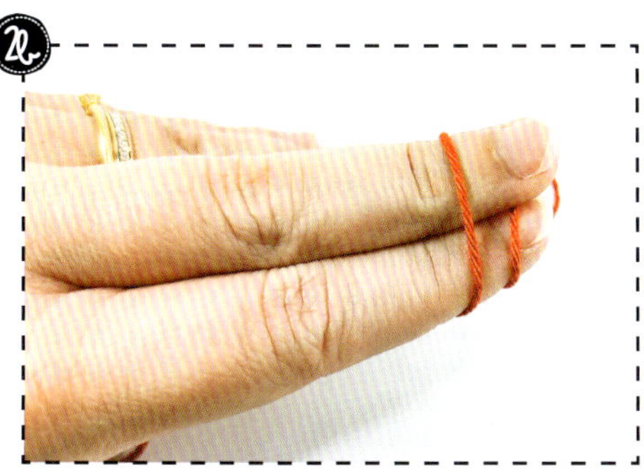

Here is another view of how to hold the yarn.

3

Run the hook under the first strand to grab the other (the one on the left).

4

Draw the yarn under the other strand, thus creating a loop on your hook.

5

Yarn over (wrap the yarn around your hook).

6

Draw the yarn you've wrapped around your hook through the loop on the hook.

7

Very gently remove the ring of yarn from your fingers so you can now work around it.

It is not easy to work with so little material in your hands, so go slowly and try not to pull on the yarn, which would close the ring.

Insert your hook through the ring.

Yarn over (wrap the yarn around your hook).

Draw the yarn you've wrapped around your hook through the ring.

Yarn over (wrap the yarn around your hook).

Draw the yarn you've wrapped around your hook through the two loops on your hook.

Here is the first single crochet on your ring. Make 5 more (6 in total), repeating Steps 8–12.

Here are the 6 single crochets that you'll have (indicated by arrows).

day 3

14

It's best to remove your hook for this next step; widen the working loop so that you don't lose it (indicated by a dot).

Then pull on the end of the yarn (indicated by an arrow).

15

Here is what you'll have after pulling the yarn. The ring can reopen, so I recommend pulling the yarn tight. Once you've made the next round, you will be able to permanently fix it in place.

Note: You still have your 6 stitches (each indicated by a dot).

16

Make a single crochet in the first stitch of your ring.

17

It is now time to place your stitch marker in the stitch you've just made so you can easily find it again. To do this, insert it through both loops and close it.

18

Now that you've marked your first stitch, make a second in the same spot to create an increase.

Once you've completed this increase, make another 5 increases in the 5 remaining stitches in the round.

In a pattern, it will be written: 6 inc (12 st).

Which means: Make 6 increases to get 12 stitches.

19

When you've finished your 6 increases (and therefore your 12 stitches), you should be at the stitch just before your stitch marker.

20

Pause for a moment to turn your work over and knot your starting yarn to fix it in place. Use a yarn needle to do this (a round-tipped needle).

21

You are now going to tackle the third round. Start by removing your stitch marker, then make a single crochet and place it again.

Once you've completed this stitch, make an increase in the following stitch.

In a pattern, it will be written: *1 sc, inc* × 6 (18 st)

Which means: Repeat the instructions between *...* 6 times in all. So if you expand that, it will be: 1 sc, 1 increase, 1 sc, 1 increase, 1 sc, 1 increase, 1 sc, 1 increase, 1 sc, 1 increase, 1 sc, 1 increase. Meaning 18 stitches.

22a

You have 18 stitches and have made three rounds: the first with 6 stitches in the magic ring (1), the second with 6 increases (2), and the last with an increase in every other stitch (3).

To make a perfect sphere: You need to have as many rounds without increases as you have with increases. You are therefore going to make two rounds of 18 single crochets so that your work straightens out.

Note: If you wanted to have a wider circle for a foundation, you would need to continue increasing by 6 for each round (24 stitches in round 4, 30 stitches in round 5, etc.)

22b

Let's take a moment to discuss the right and wrong side of a work in the round. The right side (which will be the exterior) is the one in Step 22 where you see the Vs of the stitches (which you learned to recognize on Day 2). If you see horizontal stitches (as in the photo for this step), you are on the wrong side of the work.

day 3

23

Here is what you'll have when you finish two rounds of 18 single crochets.

Note: Remember to move your stitch marker with each round.

24

Viewed from above (you can see that the starting yarn has not been worked in. This is not necessary because we will be closing the work to make a sphere).

25

Now, make a round of decreases:

1 sc, dec × 6 (12 st)

Which means: Repeat the instructions between *...* 6 times in all. So if you expand that, it will be: 1 sc, 1 decrease, 1 sc, 1 decrease, 1 sc, 1 decrease, 1 sc, 1 decrease, 1 sc, 1 decrease, 1 sc, 1 decrease. Meaning 12 stitches.

Note: Remember to move your stitch marker.

26

You are back to 12 stitches, it's time to stuff your sphere.

27

Make a last round of decreases: 6 dec (6 st)

Which means: Make 6 decreasess.

28

You are back to 6 stitches. Finish firmly stuffing the sphere. It needs to be firm because the stuffing will compress with time, so even if it seems too hard at first, this will allow the work to maintain its shape over time.

Cut the yarn, but not too short. Keep 6″ (15cm) to make closing easier.

29

To properly close the 6 last stitches, use your needle.

You are going to insert it through each front loop of your 6 stitches (indicated by dots).

30

Once the yarn is run through the 6 stitches, pull it tight.

Your sphere is now closed, you can pass the yarn under the stitches to hold it in place.

31

Here is the final product. You can make a few spheres to practice.

Tomorrow, we'll see how to start a work in an oval.

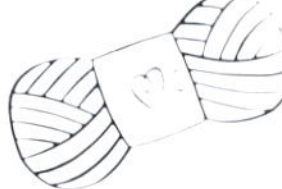

I learn to START WITH AN OVAL

MATERIALS

- E-4 crochet hook (3.50mm)
- Fine/sport weight cotton yarn
- Scissors
- Stitch marker

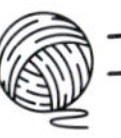

Some projects start out as an oval and not a circle, so they require that you start with a chain. This allows you to change the shape of the work, even if the increases that follow are often similar to those for a sphere.

1

Chain 6.

2

Insert your hook into the second stitch from the hook (remember: You do not work in the first stitch—the one marked with a dot) to begin your single crochets. You are therefore working your first row as you learned on Day 2.

Make 4 sc (single crochets), and leave the last one for the next step.

3

You have just done your 4 sc (each indicated by a dot). To keep your bearings, put a stitch marker in in the first stitch (the rightmost stitch).

You still have the last stitch in which you have not yet worked (indicated by an arrow).

4

Make an inc3, or a triple increase (3 single crochets in a single stitch) in the last stitch of the row.

Note: The triple increase is indicated by dots.

5

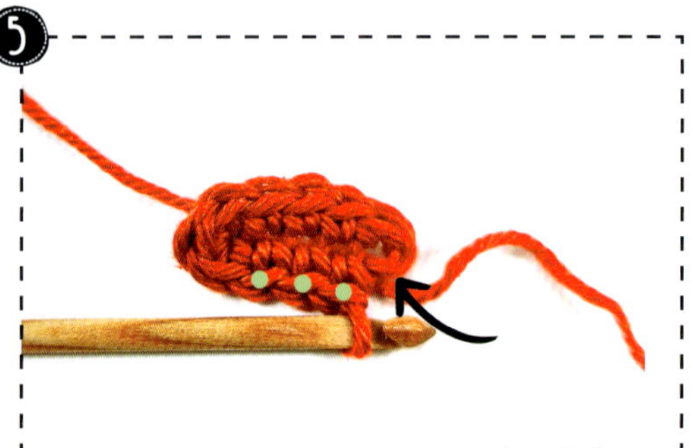

Don't turn but instead continue on the other side of the chain, making stitches to mirror the ones you've just made.

Make 3 single crochets (indicated by dots).

So you have one stitch left which has not yet been worked (indicated by an arrow)

6

In this last stitch, make an increase (indicated by dots), meaning 2 single crochets in the same stitch.

You have now finished your round.

7

Make a single crochet in the first stitch of the previous round and place your stitch marker (or move it if you already placed it in the first row).

You now have 12 stitches, you have started your first oval-shaped work.

8

You are going to work another round as you did for the sphere: *1 sc, inc* × 6 (18 st)

Here is the result once you've finished your row. You have 18 stitches.

Note: Don't forget that you already made your first single crochet when you moved your stitch marker.

THE SLIP STITCH

The slip stitch is a stitch that is only used to fasten off or close a project, or sometimes to make finer adjustments to a shape than is possible with increases and decreases. You will come across this stitch often in your creations and it's easy to do, so remember it well.

9

Remove your stitch marker and insert your hook into the stitch where it was.

10

Yarn over (wrap the yarn around your hook).

11

Draw the yarn you've wrapped around your hook through the stitch into which you inserted your hook in Step 9. You now have 2 loops on your hook.

You will now finish the movement by drawing the left loop (indicated by an arrow) through the right loop (indicated by a dot).

12

You have just completed your first slip stitch, which allows you to fasten the row off.

13

You can now pull the yarn to widen the loop and cut it (always keeping 6″ or 15cm for sewing).

FASTENING OFF IN THE ROUND OR IN AN OVAL

While it is easy to fasten off your flat work at the end of a row (you simply need to hide your yarn in the work), it is more complicated to close a round. Indeed, if you stop after the slip stitch and hide your yarn in the work, you will have a clear divide. There is a technique for making it invisible.

14

Take your yarn needle and insert it into the second stitch (indicated by an arrow) from the slip stitch (indicated by a dot).

Note: You therefore leave the middle stitch alone (indicated by a star).

15

Next return to the slip stitch (indicated by a dot) and insert your needle where the yarn comes out, then make a knot on the wrong side of your work to permanently secure the yarn.

Note: Make sure you don't make this false stitch too tight. Don't hesitate to pull a little on your work to have the same tension throughout.

16

And here is the finished work with the invisible stitching.

CROCHETING TWO LAYERS TOGETHER

You will sometimes need to crochet two pieces together to close an amigurumi, or even to make ears in two colors. In these situations, the pattern will always give instructions for which stitch to use and it's usually the single crochet.

17

Repeat Steps 1–8 (stop before making the slip stitch, which you will not do here).

Next, position the two ovals with wrong sides together (see Day 3 for how to differentiate between the right and wrong sides).

18

Once the ovals are positioned, you are going to make a single crochet: Insert your hook into the first stitch of the first oval then into that of the second (so across the full width). Yarn over and draw the yarn through both layers, then yarn over again to draw the yarn through both loops on your hook.

19

You have made your first single crochet and have begun to join the two ovals.

You will now make single crochets all around the ovals (so 18 single crochets in total).

20

This is what you will have. All that's left is to fasten off invisibly as explained in Steps 14–16.

21

Here is what you will have when this stitch is complete.

day 5

I learn about FRONT LOOP AND BACK LOOP

MATERIALS

- E-4 crochet hook (3.50mm)
- Fine/sport weight cotton yarn
- Scissors
- Stitch marker

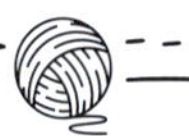

On Day 2, you learned to insert your hook under both loops of a stitch when crocheting a new one. However, sometimes you need to crochet with only the front loop or back loop of the stitch in the previous row. This is essentially done for aesthetic purposes, to shape your work, or even to leave stitches on hold until they're worked later (see Days 4 and 15 with the Teddy Tree project).

1

Return to Step 21 on Day 2: Chain 10 stitches, then make two rows of 9 single crochets.

2

Now make single crochets, inserting your hook under only the front loop of the stitches in the previous row (indicated by green dots).

Do this along the entire row.

Once your row is finished, there will be no visual difference on the side facing you, because you've worked in the front loops.

If you turn your work over, however, the unworked back loops are visible (indicated by green arrows) and form and line.

Now work in the back loops (indicated by green dots) to make the single crochets of the following row and see the difference (on a piece worked flat, in rows).

This time, the unworked loops are visible on the front of your work (indicated by green arrows) because you've worked in the back loops.

And you can see that they are visible on the back as well because it creates a furrow (indicated by a green arrow).

This allows you to see that the effect is different depending on the method.

I make CAMILLA CAMPFIRE

THE LOGS—PART 1

MATERIALS

- D-3 crochet hook (3.00mm)
- Fine/sport weight cotton yarn – Brown ≈38 yards (35m)
- Scissors/yarn needle
- Stitch marker
- Stuffing

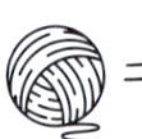

PATTERN Logs / Make 3 / Brown

FIRST PART

rnd 0 = Start with a magic ring
rnd 1 = 6 sc in the ring (6 st)
rnd 2 = 6 inc (12 st)
rnd 3 = [BL] 12 sc
rnd 4–21 (18 rnds) = 12 sc

Finish with one sl st, cut, and work the yarn in. Make three logs in all.

SECOND PART

rnd 0 = Start with a magic ring
rnd 1 = 6 sc in the ring (6 st)
rnd 2 = 6 inc (12 st)

Finish with one sl st and cut the yarn, leaving enough length for sewing. Firmly stuff the log, then sew on the circle you've just made to close it. Do this three times (one brown circle per log).

day 5

THE LOGS, STEP BY STEP

Let's go over the pattern together. You'll be putting Day 3's lesson into practice.

FIRST PART

Rounds 0–1: Start with a magic ring and make 6 single crochets in it. Remember to place your stitch marker so you don't lose the beginning of the round.

Round 2: Make your first round of increases to go from 6 stitches to 12. The number in parentheses tells you how many stitches you need to have at the end of your round. It is generally included for rounds when the number of stitches varies (increases / decreases).

Round 3: Just like our lesson today, you're going to make a round of 12 single crochets working in the back loops only. This allows you to create the corner at the end of the log.

Rounds 4–21: Simply make rounds of 12 stitches to create the log's length. Remember to stuff it regularly (and firmly, as explained on Day 3).

Once these rounds are complete, make a slip stitch, then fasten off as explained on Day 4. Do this two more times to make a total of three logs. Stuff firmly.

Note: You'll note that I've chosen to make a second part to "close" the log rather than using decreases. This is an aesthetic choice, because decreasing from 12 stitches will not create as neat a circle as with increases. I've therefore favored aesthetics and bit of sewing.

SECOND PART

Rounds 0–1: Start with a magic ring and make 6 stitches in it. Remember to place your stitch marker so you don't lose the beginning of the round.

Round 2: Make your first round of increases to go from 6 stitches to 12.

Once these two rounds are complete, make a slip stitch and leave 8″ (20cm) of yarn to do your sewing before cutting. Do this two more times to have a total of 3 circles.

SEWING

Get your yarn needle, place the second part on the first, and sew, inserting your needle under both loops of the stitches on the first part and under the back loop of the stitches on the second part.

Ta da! You have just made your three logs, you can leave them loose or else hold them in place with a few tiny stitches, ready to receive Camilla tomorrow.

I learn about PICOTS

MATERIALS

- E-4 crochet hook (3.50mm)
- Fine/sport weight cotton yarn
- Scissors
- Stitch marker

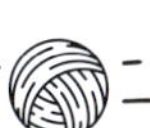

Before making the second part of Camilla Campfire, you'll learn how to do picots, then how to place safety eyes. Once you've acquired these skills, you can finish your very first amigurumi.

1

Return to Step 21 on Day 2: Chain 10 then make two rows of 9 single crochets.

2

Make a slip stitch (Day 4) in the first stitch.

Note: This is done to move in from the edge and to make working easier, but it's not part of the picot.

3a

Begin your picot: Chain three.

3b When you turn your work, you can see the three back "bumps" of the three chain stitches you've just made (indicated by arrows).

4 Insert your hook into the back loop of the first chain stitch (the furthest on the left in Step 3b).

5 Yarn over (wrap the yarn around your hook).

6 Draw the yarn through the two loops on your hook: Thus you have just made a slip stitch in the back loop of your first chain stitch.

7 Reposition your work in the right direction and do a slip stitch in the next stitch.

You have just made your first picot.

8 Make two slip stitches (to space out the picots as in the upcoming pattern).

Make a second picot: Chain three, one slip stitch in the back bump of the first chain, and then make one slip stitch in the next stitch in the row.

Once the second picot is made, finish your row by making two slip stitches, one picot, then one last slip stitch.

And here is what you'll have when you're done.

SAFETY EYES

Safety eyes are a good solution for amigurumi because they can be attached accurately and securely. However, if your amigurumi is intended for a small child, I would always recommend embroidering rather than attaching eyes, even safety ones.

Safety eyes are made up of two parts: the eye with a notched stem, and the washer to attach it. They must always be placed BEFORE your close your work!

1

Insert the eyes in your work.

Note: The spot where eyes should be placed is always specified in the pattern, along with the spacing between the eyes. When it says "six stitches between the eyes," you need to place the first eye, then count six stitches and place the second.

In this photo, there are 4 stitches in between, but once placed, the eyes obscure part of these stitches, so make sure you count because it's not visually obvious.

2

Turn your work over to reach the notched stems.

3

Push the washers as far as you can. Ta da! You've attached the eyes for your amigurumi.

I make CAMILLA CAMPFIRE

THE FLAMES—PART 2

MATERIALS

- D-3 crochet hook (3.00mm)
- Fine/sport weight cotton yarn – Yellow ≈ 38 yards (35m)
- Scissors/yarn needle
- Stitch marker
- Stuffing

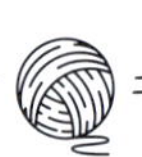

PATTERN **Body** / Yellow

rnd 0 = Start by chaining 6, turn
rnd 1 = 4 sc, inc3 (in the last stitch of your chain)–Don't turn but continue on the other side of the chain (start with an oval)–3 sc, inc (12 st)
rnd 2 = *1 sc, inc* × 6 (18 st)
rnd 3 = 1 sc, inc, *2 sc, inc* × 5, 1 sc (24 st)
rnd 4 = *3 sc, inc* × 6 (30 st)
rnd 5 = 2 sc, inc, *4 sc, inc* × 5, 2 sc (36 st)
rnd 6–12 (7 rnds) = 36 sc–Place the safety eyes between rnds 9 and 10 (6 stitches in between)
rnd 13 = 2 sc, dec, *4 sc, dec* × 5, 2 sc (30 st)
rnd 14 = *3 sc, dec* × 6 (24 st)
rnd 15–17 (3 rnds) = 24 sc
STUFF CAMILLA AND MAKE ROUND 18 THROUGH BOTH LAYERS OF THE WORK (so 12 doubled stitches)
rnd 18 = 1 sl st, *p, 3 sl st* × 3, p, 2 sl st
Cut and work the yarn in.

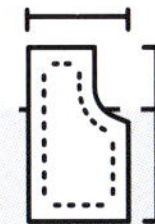

PATTERN **Arm** / Yellow

r 0 = Start by chaining 6, turn
r 1 = 5 sc

Cut the yarn, leaving enough length to sew the arms on each side of Camilla Campfire, between rounds 8 and 10.

CAMILLA CAMPFIRE'S BODY, STEP BY STEP

BODY

Let's go over the pattern together. You'll be putting Day 4's lesson into practice.

Rounds 0–1: Start by chaining 6 then make your first round, working around the chain. Remember to place your stitch marker so you don't lose the beginning of the round.

Rounds 2–5: Make four rounds of increase to widen the base of Camilla Campfire.

Important: You will notice that rounds 3 and 5 don't incorporate increases in the same way as rounds 2 and 4. This is to avoid having increases in the same spot, which would cause your work to look like a lozenge rather than an oval. You will still add the same number of stitches in the end, that doesn't change.

Rounds 6–12: These are "normal" rounds with 36 single crochets in each round. Don't forget to place the safety eyes between rows 9 and 10 with 6 stitches between them.

Rounds 13 and 14: Ease into your decreases.

Rounds 15–16 and 17: These are "normal" rounds with 24 single crochets in each round.

Round 18: Fold the amigurumi in half to close it, inserting your hook through both layers (Day 4), and make your picots. Don't worry if you make one extra or one too few, it's not a big deal, it'll just give it a more flame-like quality. Have fun with it!

Once round 18 is finished, cut the yarn and work it in.

ARMS

Row 0: Start by chaining 6 and turn.

Row 1: Make a "normal" row of 5 single crochets.

Cut the yarn, leaving a tail of about 6″ (15cm) before drawing it through the loop on your hook.

SEWING

Use the 6″ (15cm) tail to sew the arms onto Camilla Campfire's sides between rows 8 and 10. Feel free to use pins to place them correctly and help you out. So the arms stay along the sides, you can sew them onto several stitches.

Advice AFTER YOUR FIRST AMIGURUMI

You've just finished Camilla Campfire, your first amigurumi. It is now time to assess how you feel and how your project has turned out. Can you see the stuffing? Is it too loose, or too tight? Are you stuck on a particular technique? Let's figure out the solution together.

First off, don't be too hard on yourself if your work isn't perfect. If this is your very first amigurumi, it's to be expected that it won't necessarily look like the photos. It could turn out to be your lucky charm for the rest of this course, so take good care of it.

When it comes to technique, we can look at several points:

—If you find that your stitches are irregular or that you're missing stitches, you should take the time to work through the first days again. For example, start by making rectangles of single crochets to make a little pouch. Any project that allows you to crochet without too much consideration is perfect for practicing. It may be that you haven't found your movements yet and that's why you're getting stuck.

—Does Camilla seem too tight? This is why I had you work with a larger-sized hook for your lessons on Days 2–4. Try out the E-4 (3.50mm) hook instead and use it for all the other amigurumi.

—Does Camilla seem too loose? You have two options: Use a smaller crochet hook (C-2 or 2.50mm) or else change how you make your stitches. I recommend starting with this second option. Here's how to make X-shaped single crochets, which will tighten up your work:

1a

Normally, after you insert your hook through the stitch, you would yarn over to wrap the yarn around your hook.

Note: This photo is just for comparison, you will begin with 1b.

1b

To make the X-shaped single crochet, you're not going to wrap your yarn, but rather draw it through the stitch as it is.

Note: Before starting this row, I chained 10 then made two rows of "normal" single crochets. Feel free to do the same so you can better compare.

2

You have two loops on your hook, as you would with a normal single crochet.

3

Grab the yarn again and draw it through the stitch. Don't wrap it, just take it as it is.

4

You have finished your first X-shaped single crochet.

5

Continue to make X-shaped single crochets the length of your row, drawing the yarn through without wrapping it around the hook.

Here is the result.

For the first two rows, there are normal single crochets and on the last, the X-shaped single crochets. This name derives from the shape of the stitch, and you will see that your row has a much tighter finish, which may help you.

—Unsure about how to hold your hook or your yarn? There is no one-size-fits-all way to hold your hook or yarn, you have to find what works for you. Don't forget that it's the hook that goes to meet the yarn and not the other way around, so your left hand barely moves (or the opposite, if you're left-handed). However, here are the most common positions:

Hook hold—1

You can hold your hook like a pencil.

Hook hold—2

Or like a knife. This may change with experience, that's normal.

Yarn hold—1

The yarn can be simply passed over your index finger (and the rest held by your other fingers).

Yarn hold—2

You can also stretch the yarn out with your index finger to make hooking it easier (the rest of the yarn still held by your other fingers).

—If the problem comes from sewing, you need to take your time and use pins. Don't worry if it's not perfectly symmetrical, nothing and nobody ever is! **Concerned about working your yarn back in?** Keep it simple using a yarn needle.

Working in the yarn

With a yarn needle, run the yarn under a half dozen stitches and cut.

For our purposes, simply stick the yarn into the amigurumi to save yourself the bother (after running it under a few stitches).

Sewing elements on a base—1

You learned on Day 4 how to crochet together two pieces of the same size, but more often you will need to sew elements onto a base (for example, arms onto an amigurumi's body).

Tip: Run the needle under a stitch on the base.

Sewing elements on a base—2

Then run your needle through the element you're sewing.

Sewing elements on a base—3

Next, sew back through the element before returning to your base. Continue in this way all along the piece: one stitch of the base, one stitch of the addition, one stitch of the base, one stitch of the addition, etc.

—Questions about stuffing? I always recommend stuffing firmly. Even if the amigurumi seems too hard at first, you have to remember that stuffing compresses over time, so if you don't use enough, the shape won't hold for long.

Now that you've taken the time to study your first amigurumi, we can move on to the next lessons.

I learn about JACQUARD AND COLOR CHANGES

MATERIALS

- E-4 crochet hook (3.50mm)
- Fine/sport weight cotton yarn
- Scissors
- Stitch marker

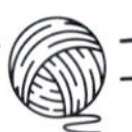

Jacquard, also called tapestry crochet, allows you to create patterns in your work by changing colors several times in the same round (or row). The most difficult aspect of this technique is the yarn tension, which is why you'll be shown two different methods of running your thread on the back. I recommend trying both to figure out which one works best for you; so take your time practicing.

1

Redo the lesson from Day 3.

Make a magic ring then a second round of 6 increases to go from 6 to 12 stitches.

Lastly, make a third round increasing on every other stitch to go from 12 to 18 stitches: *1 sc, inc* × 6 (18 st).

2

On the fourth round, you are going to change colors to make a jacquard pattern.

Make two single crochets, then start to make a third: Insert your hook through the stitch in the previous round, yarn over, draw the yarn through the stitch.

However, stop here, without completing the final step.

3

Draw the second color yarn (beige) through the loops to complete your single crochet. This will allow you to make a clean color change.

Note: This yarn will be very loose at first, don't worry about it and continue crocheting, you will tighten it later when securing the yarn ends.

FIRST METHOD

4

Make two single crochets with the new color (beige) before stopping again at the last step of the third one (as you did in Step 2).

5a

Take back up the yarn of the first color (orange) to finish your stitch.

5b

For the moment, don't try to secure your yarn, simply take it up again without adding tension. You can even leave it loose like in the photo.

6

Start again at Step 2 to make your three new single crochets in orange, then continue to finish the round: changing color every three stitches.

Note: Don't forget that the color change starts with the last step of a single crochet in the previous color.

7a

Here is what you'll have at the end of the round. It is possible that your work may come in slightly (because you're no longer increasing) so don't hesitate to flatten it.

Here is the wrong side of your work with the visible yarn tails.

Note: This is not a problem with amigurumi because this part will not be visible. But if your work is reversible, you need to run the yarn through your work to hide it.

Here's the method...

5

The new yarn (beige) is therefore holding the second (orange) in place along the work. Make sure not to pull on the orange yarn, simply let it run along under your stitches.

Make your three beige stitches (in total) the same way.

7

SECOND METHOD

4

Rework through Step 3 to try out the method of hiding your non-working yarn.

Once you've drawn the new color yarn (beige) through the work, run the first color yarn (orange) next to the stitches of the previous round to trap it within your new stitches.

Insert your hook through the stitch (the orange yarn is on top of the hook along with the two loops of the stitch), yarn over, then draw the yarn through the stitch.

6

Once you've made your three beige stitches, move on to three new orange stitches, this time running the beige yarn under the orange.

Sometimes the yarn can go on top of the stitches in the previous round, this will make holding the yarn easier.

Continue to make your round, alternating three single crochets of each color.

8a. The result on the right side of the work is identical to the first method.

8b. The wrong side of the work is much "neater," which is needed for a reversible project.

However, if you feel more comfortable with the first method, don't force yourself to use the second, because the wrong side of the work is rarely visible with amigurumi once stuffed.

CHANGING COLORS IN THE ROUND

There are myriad ways of neatly changing colors in the round and avoiding the sort of "step" that is created when using the jacquard technique. If you want to prevent the new color from encroaching on a round of the previous color:

1. Make a magic ring, then a second row with 6 increases to go from 6 to 12 stitches.

Next make a third round, increasing on every other stitch to go from 12 to 18 stitches: *1 sc, 1 inc* × 6 (18 st).

Once this is done, fasten off your round as you learned on Day 4. Then make a slip knot on your hook with the new color (beige).

2. With the new color, insert your hook through a stitch in the previous round.

3

Make your first single crochet then continue your round, increasing to go from 18 to 24 stitches, like so:

1 sc, inc, *2 sc, inc* × 5, 1 sc (24 st)

Note: Don't forget your stitch marker if you need it.

4

Once you've finished the round, simply continue by inserting your hook through the first beige stitch and make a second round (remembering to increase), like so:

3 sc, inc × 6 (30 st)

5

You now have three rounds of orange and two rounds of beige. There is no dividing line between the two, you have achieved a clean color change.

If you needed to return to the orange yarn, you would fasten off as seen on Day 4 before starting again at Step 1.

Don't hesitate to practice jacquard and changing colors. This will also allow you to better understand increasing in rounds (which will always be by sixes because you started with 6 stitches).

Tomorrow, you're going to add colors to Kyle Campfire!

I make KYLE CAMPFIRE

Now that you've practiced your jacquard and color changes, you can give more personality to Kyle Campfire by combining colors. Feel free to choose whichever colors you like, the materials I use are intended as a guide.

MATERIALS

- D-3 crochet hook (3.00mm)
- Fine/sport weight cotton yarn
  - Red ≈ 22 yards (20m)
  - Orange ≈ 11 yards (10m)
  - Yellow ≈ 5 yards (5m)
  - Brown ≈ 27 yards (25m)
  - Cream ≈ 11 yards (10m)
- 2 safety eyes, 1/4″ (6mm)
- Stuffing
- Scissors/yarn needle
- Stitch marker

PATTERN **Logs / Make 3 /** Brown and Cream

PART 1

rnd 0 = (Cream) Start with a magic ring
rnd 1 = 6 sc in the ring (6 st)
rnd 2 = 6 inc (12 st)
rnd 3 = [BL] (Brown) 12 sc
rnd 4–21 (18 rnds) = 12 sc

Finish with a sl st, cut the yarn and work it in. Make three logs, then:

PART 2

rnd 0 = (Cream) Start with a magic ring
rnd 1 = 6 sc in the ring (6 st)
rnd 2 = 6 inc (12 st)

Finish with a sl st and cut the yarn, leaving enough length for sewing. Stuff the log firmly, then sew on the circle you have just made to close it. Do this three times (one Cream circle per log).

PATTERN **Body** /Red, Orange, and Yellow

rnd 0 = (Red) Start by chaining 6, turn
rnd 1 = 4 sc, inc3 (in the last stitch of your chain)—Do not turn, but instead continue along the other side of the chain (start with an oval)—3 sc, inc (12 st)
rnd 2 = *1 sc, inc* × 6 (18 st)
rnd 3 = 1 sc, inc, *2 sc, inc* × 5, 1 sc (24 st)
rnd 4 = *3 sc, inc* × 6 (30 st)
rnd 5 = 2 sc, inc, *4 sc, inc* × 5, 2 sc (36 st)
rnd 6–9 (4 rnds) = 36 sc
JACQUARD ON ROUNDS 10 AND 11
rnd 10 = *(Red) 3 sc, (Orange) 1 sc* × 9 (36 st)
rnd 11 = (Red) 1 sc, *(Red) 1 sc, (Orange) 3 sc* × 8, (Red) 1 sc, (Orange) 2 sc (36 st)—Place the eyes between rnds 9 and 10 (with 6 stitches in between)
rnd 12 = (Orange) 36 st
rnd 13 = 2 sc, dec, *4 sc, dec* × 5, 2 sc (30 st)
rnd 14 = *3 sc, dec* × 6 (24 st)
JACQUARD ON ROUNDS 15 AND 16
rnd 15 = *(Orange) 3 sc, (Yellow) 1 sc* × 6 (24 st)
rnd 16 = (Orange) 1 sc, *(Orange) 1 sc, (Yellow) 3 sc* × 5, (Orange) 1 sc, (Yellow) 2 sc (24 st)
rnd 17 = (Yellow) 24 sc)
Tr. 17 = (Yellow) 24 ms
STUFF KYLE AND MAKE ROUND 18 THROUGH BOTH LAYERS OF THE WORK (so 12 doubled stitches)
rnd 18 = 1 sl st, *p, 3 sl st* × 3, p, 2 sl st.
Cut the yarn and work it in.

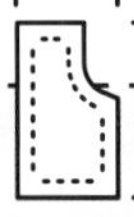

PATTERN **Arms** /Red

r 0 = Start by chaining 6, turn
r 1 = 5 sc
Cut the yarn, leaving enough length to sew the arms on either side of the fire, between rounds 8 and 10.

day 9

COLORFUL KYLE CAMPFIRE, STEP BY STEP

You are now going to create the first part of your amigurumi: the logs.

THE LOGS, STEP BY STEP

Let's go over the pattern together. This time, you will be putting Day 8 into practice, because you've already done this pattern with a single color. Colors are indicated in parentheses before the stitches you need to make. If there is no color indicated, it means you should continue with the same color.

Part 1

Rounds 0–1: Start with a magic ring in cream with 6 stitches in it. Remember to place your stitch marker so you don't lose the beginning of your round.

Round 2: Make your first round of increases to go from 6 to 12 stitches, then cut the yarn and fasten off like you learned on Day 4 and again on Day 8 with color changes.

Round 3: Make a round of 12 single crochets in brown, using only the back loop. This will allow you to create the corner at the end of the log.

Rounds 4–21: Simply make rounds of 12 stitches each to create the length of the log. Remember to stuff regularly (it needs to be firm as explained on Day 3).

Once these rounds are complete, make a slip stitch then fasten off the final round as explained on Day 4. Do this two more times to have a total of three logs. Stuff firmly.

Part 2

Rounds 0–1: Start with a magic ring in cream with 6 stitches in it. Remember to place your stitch marker so you don't lose the beginning of your round.

Round 2: Make your first round of increases to go from 6 to 12 stitches.

Once these two rounds are complete, make a slip stitch and leave 8″ (20cm) of yarn when cutting to do the sewing. Repeat another two times to have a total of three circles.

Sewing

Take your yarn needle, position the second part on the first part, and sew, inserting your needle under both loops of the stitches on the first part and under just the back loop of the stitches on the second part.

And there you have it, you have just finished your three logs. You can leave them loose or make a few small stitches to hold them together as for the first logs.

KYLE CAMPFIRE'S BODY, STEP BY STEP

Flames

Let's go over the pattern together. Take all the time you need, because you're going to have to work four rounds in jacquard. If you accidentally do the wrong number stitches of any color, it's not a big deal. Just relax and off we go!

Rounds 0–1: Start by chaining 6 in red, then make your first round worked around the chain. Remember to place your stitch marker so you don't lose the beginning of your round.

Rounds 2–9: The bulk of Kyle's body is made in red, done just like the yellow version.

Rounds 10–11: These are the rounds that require the most focus because you will be making your first jacquard pattern to change progressively from red to orange. The color of the stitch you need to make is indicated in parentheses just before the stitch or stitches.

*Example: For round 10, you do: *3 red single crochets, 1 orange single crochet* and repeat that 9 times in all.*

Don't forget to place your safety eyes between rounds 9 and 10 with 6 stitches between them.

Rounds 12–14: Three rounds in orange as your begin your decreases.

Rounds 15–16: Two jacquard rounds to change from orange to yellow, as explained for rounds 10 and 11.

Round 17: A "normal" round of single crochets in yellow.

Round 18: Fold the amigurumi in half to close, inserting your hook through both layers (Day 4) to make your picots.

Once round 18 is complete, cut the yarn and work it in.

Arms

Row 0: Start by chaining 6 in red, then turn.

Row 1: Make a "simple" row of 5 single crochets.

Cut the yarn, leaving 6″ (15cm) before drawing it through the loop on your hook.

Sewing

Use those 6″ (15cm) of yarn to sew the arms onto the side of the flames between rounds 8 and 10. Don't hesitate to use pins to accurately position them and to help you out. You can sew in several stitches so that the arms stay along the body.

And there you have Camilla Campfire's colorful twin! With these two, campfires will never be the same. What do you think?

day 10

I learn

THE HALF DOUBLE AND DOUBLE CROCHETS

MATERIALS

- E-4 crochet hook (3.50mm)
- Fine/sport weight cotton yarn
- Scissors
- Stitch marker

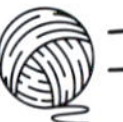

Half double and double crochets are rarely used when making amigurumi because the larger the stitch, the more open they are, so the stuffing can come out. However, they are still worth learning as they can help to give form to certain parts of an amigurumi and also to create more complex stitches. Take the time to really understand how they work, which is fairly logical: The larger the stitches, the more steps and yarn they involve.

HALF DOUBLE CROCHET

1

Repeat the steps from Day 2: Chain 10, then do two rows of single crochets.

Because you will be making half double crochets—larger stitches—chain 2 at the end of the row (instead of only one) before you turn. This will allow you to start at the same height as the half double crochets.

2

Turn your work, then yarn over (wrap the yarn around your hook).

3

Next insert your hook through the third stitch from your hook (thus skipping over the two chain stitches before inserting your hook through the first stitch of the previous row).

4

Yarn over (wrap the yarn around your hook).

5

Draw the yarn you've wrapped around your hook through the stitch into which you inserted your hook in Step 3.

You now have three loops on your hook.

6

Yarn over (wrap the yarn around your hook).

7

Draw the yarn you've wrapped around your hook through all three loops.

You have just made your first half double crochet.

8

Continue following these steps along the whole row to make your 9 half double crochets (the chain stitches at the beginning of the row don't count).

DOUBLE CROCHET

1

Repeat the steps from Day 2: Chain 10, then do two rows of single crochets.

Because you will be making double crochets, chain 3 at the end of the row before you turn. This will allow you to start at the same height as the double crochets.

2

Turn your work, then yarn over (wrap the yarn around your hook).

3

Next insert your hook through the fourth stitch from your hook (thus skipping over the three chain stitches before inserting your hook through the first stitch of the previous row).

4

Yarn over (wrap the yarn around your hook).

5

Draw the yarn you've wrapped around your hook through the stitch into which you inserted your hook in Step 3. You now have three loops on your hook.

6

Yarn over (wrap the yarn around your hook).

Draw the yarn you've wrapped around your hook through the two loops on the left (leaving the last one on the right).

You now have two loops on your hook.

Yarn over (wrap the yarn around your hook).

Draw the yarn you've wrapped around your hook through the last two loops.

You have just made your first double crochet.

Continue following these steps along the whole row to make your 9 double crochets (the chain stitches at the beginning of the row don't count).

Note: Double crochets do not create a very straight edge for your work; therefore, if you're working flat, I recommend adding a border to hide this.

Here is a photo so you can compare the sizes of the different stitches.

The single crochet rows are in green, the half doubles in blue, and the double crochets in yellow.

Go ahead and make several rows with the different stitches. You will need to have a good grasp of half double crochets for Sally Squirrel's tail, then double crochets for *Bradley Bear*.

day 11

I make SALLY SQUIRREL

PART 1

MATERIALS

- D-3 crochet hook (3.00mm)
- Fine/sport weight cotton yarn
  - Orange ≈ 88 yards (80m)
  - White ≈ 11 yards (10m)
- Stuffing
- Yarn needle/scissors/pins
- 2 safety eyes, 1/4″ (6mm)
- Stitch marker

You now have everything you need to know in order to start a larger amigurumi like Sally Squirrel. Today you will make her body and belly. Tomorrow you'll work the smaller elements.

PATTERN **Body** / Orange

rnd 0 = Start with a magic ring
rnd 1 = 6 sc in the ring (6 st)
rnd 2 = 6 inc (12 st)
rnd 3 = *1 sc, inc* × 6 (18 st)
rnd 4 = 1 sc, inc, *2 sc, inc* × 5, 1 sc (24 st)
rnd 5 = *3 sc, inc* × 6 (30 st)
rnd 6 = 30 sc
rnd 7 = 2 sc, inc, *4 sc, inc* × 5, 2 sc (36 st)
rnd 8 = 36 sc
rnd 9 = *5 sc, inc* × 6 (42 st)
rnd 10–25 (16 rnds) = 42 sc
→ Place the eyes between rounds 10 and 11 with 7 stitches in between
rnd 26 = *5 sc, dec* × 6 (36 st)
rnd 27 = 36 sc
rnd 28 = 2 sc, dec, *4 sc, dec* × 5, 2 sc (30 st → Remember to start stuffing
rnd 29 = *3 sc, dec* × 6 (24 st)
rnd 30 = 1 sc, dec, *2 sc, dec* × 5, 1 sc (18 st)
rnd 31 = *1 sc, dec* × 6 (12 st)
rnd 32 = 6 dec (6 st)

Stuff firmly. Cut the yarn and, using a yarn needle, run it through the 6 remaining stitches, tighten, and work it in.

PATTERN **Belly** / White

rnd 0 = Start by chaining 6, turn
rnd 1 = 4 sc, inc3 (in the last stitch of your chain)–Do not turn, but instead continue onto the other side of the chain (starting with an oval)–3 sc, inc (12 st)
rnd 2 = *1 sc, inc* × 6 (18 st)
rnd 3 = 1 sc, inc, *2 sc, inc* × 5, 1 sc (24 st)
rnd 4 = *3 sc, inc* × 6 (30 st)
rnd 5 = 2 sc, inc, *4 sc, inc* × 5, 2 sc (36 st)

Finish with a sl st and cut the yarn. Don't forget to leave enough length for sewing (see remaining steps).

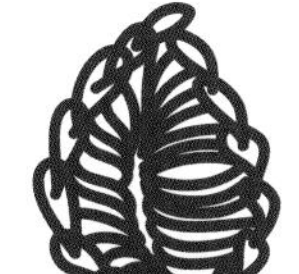

SALLY SQUIRREL'S BODY, STEP BY STEP

Rounds 0–1: Start with a magic ring in orange with 6 single crochets in the ring. Remember to place your stitch marker so you don't lose the beginning of your round.

Rounds 2–9: Increase the number of stitches in your amigurumi (except in rounds 6 and 8) in order to obtain the desired circumference for the body.

Rounds 10–25: These are "normal" rounds where you simply make 42 single crochets in each round to lengthen the body. Place the safety eyes once you get to round 14 or 15 (you can't place them between rounds 10 and 11 right away because you need some material to hold them in place).

Rounds 26–32: Decrease the stitches in your amigurumi (except in round 27) to close it. Remember to start stuffing near round 28 before completely and firmly stuffing just before round 32.

Once these rounds are complete, use your yarn needle to sew the yarn through the 6 remaining stitches, tighten, and work the yarn in (see Day 3).

SALLY SQUIRREL'S BELLY, STEP BY STEP

Rounds 0–1: Start by chaining 6 in white, then make your first round around the chain. Remember to place your stitch marker so you don't lose the beginning of your round.

Rounds 2–5: Increase with each round to obtain 36 stitches in all.

Once these rounds are complete, make a slip stitch and leave 12″ (30cm) of yarn for sewing before cutting.

I recommend waiting until you've made all the elements before you start sewing, so set the belly aside for now.

See you tomorrow for the arms, legs, ears, snout, and tail!

I make SALLY SQUIRREL

PART 2

MATERIALS

- D-3 crochet hook (3.00mm)
- Fine/sport weight cotton yarn
  - Orange ≈ 88 yards (80m)
  - White ≈ 11 yards (10m)
- Stuffing
- Yarn needle/scissors/pins
- 2 safety eyes, 1/4" (6mm)
- Stitch marker

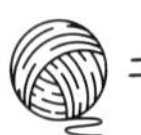

Today you are going to create the different elements that comprise Sally Squirrel. Just because these pieces are small does not mean that they're easy, so take your time. You are making your second amigurumi, so now I will only explain the more complex elements or new stitches in the step-by-step instructions.

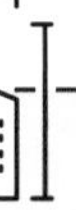

PATTERN **Arms / Make 2 /** Orange

rnd 0 = Start with a magic ring
rnd 1 = 6 sc in the ring (6 st)
rnd 2 = *1 sc, inc* × 3 (9 st)
rnd 3–8 (6 rnds) = 9 sc
rnd 9 = *1 sc, dec* × 3 (6 st)

Stuff loosely. Cut the yarn and, using a yarn needle, run it through the 6 remaining stitches and tighten. Don't forget to leave enough length for sewing (see remaining steps).

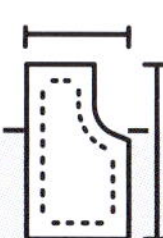

PATTERN **Snout** / White

rnd 0 = Start with a magic ring
rnd 1 = 6 sc in the ring (6 st)
rnd 2 = 6 inc (12 st)
rnd 3 = 12 sc
rnd 4 = *1 sc, inc* × 6 (18 st)

Stuff firmly, finish with a sl st, cut the yarn. Don't forget to leave enough length for sewing (see remaining steps).

PATTERN **Legs / Make 2 /** Orange

rnd 0 = Start with a magic ring
rnd 1 = 4 sc in the ring (4 st)
rnd 2 = 4 inc (8 st)
rnd 3 = 8 sc (8 st)
rnd 4 = *1 sc, inc* × 4 (12 st)
rnd 5–8 (4 rnds) = 12 sc—Remember to start stuffing
rnd 9 = *1 sc, dec* × 4 (8 st)
rnd 10 = 8 sc

Stuff loosely. Cut the yarn and, using a yarn needle, run it through the 8 remaining stitches and tighten. Don't forget to leave enough length for sewing (see remaining steps).

PATTERN **Tail /** Orange

rnd 0 = Start with a magic ring
rnd 1 = 6 sc in the ring (6 st)
rnd 2 = 6 inc (12 st)
rnd 3 = *1 sc, inc* × 6 (18 st)
rnd 4 = 1 sc, inc, *2 sc, inc* × 5, 1 sc (24 st)
rnd 5–7 (3 rnds) = 24 sc
rnd 8–10 (3 rnds) = 12 sl st, 12 hdc
rnd 11 = 12 sl st, 12 sc
rnd 12–20 (9 rnds) = 24 sc—Remember to start stuffing
rnd 21 = 1 sc, dec, *2 sc, dec* × 5, 1 sc (18 st)
rnd 22 = 18 sc
rnd 23 = *1 sc, dec* × 6 (12 st)
rnd 24 = 12 sc
rnd 25 = 6 dec (6 st)

Stuff firmly. Cut the yarn and, using a yarn needle, run it through the 6 remaining stitches and tighten. Don't forget to leave enough length for sewing (see remaining steps).

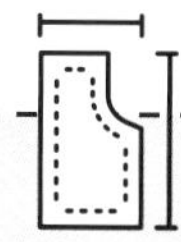

PATTERN **Ears / Make 2 /** Orange

rnd 0 = Start with a magic ring
rnd 1 = 4 sc in the ring (4 st)
rnd 2 = 4 sc
rnd 3 = 4 inc (8 st)
rnd 4 = *1 sc, inc* × 4 (12 st)
rnd 5 = 1 sc, inc, *2 sc, inc* × 3, 1 sc (16 st)
rnd 6–8 (3 rnds) = 16 sc
rnd 9 = 1 sc, dec, *2 sc, dec* × 3, 1 sc (12 st)
rnd 10 = *1 sc, dec* × 4 (8 st)
rnd 11 = 4 dec (4 st)

There is no need to stuff, finish with a sl st, cut the yarn. Don't forget to leave enough length for sewing (see remaining steps).

Next take two bits of yarn, make a knot, and thread them through from the inside to come out at the tip of the ear (the knot will prevent them from coming out). Brush them to separate the strands.

REMAINING STEPS

All of this is provided as a guide, you can do however you please.

Ears/Body Assembly

Fold the ears in half to create a hollow and stitch together. Next, position them between rounds 4 and 6 on each side of the head. So they remain straight, sew them to several rounds along the head.

Snout/Body Assembly

The top of the snout is positioned at the same level as the eyes. Center it. Stitch in red to make the nose (see photo).

Belly/Body Assembly

The belly is placed one round below the snout and goes down to the legs.

Arms/Body Assembly

The arms are positioned between rounds 15 and 19 on either side of the body.

Legs/Body Assembly

The legs are positioned between rounds 30 and 26 in a V shape. Pay attention to her stability (attach the tail with pins to make sure everything is balanced).

Tail/Body Assembly

The tail is positioned starting at round 30 and is sewn along the squirrel's back up to round 22.

SALLY SQUIRREL'S LEGS, ARMS, AND SNOUT, STEP BY STEP

By now you know starting in the round and making rounds of increases, simple single crochets, then decreases. Don't forget to always keep 6″–8″ (15–20cm) of yarn for the sewing steps, stuff firmly and set aside with the belly. You will do all the sewing at the end.

SALLY SQUIRREL'S TAIL, STEP BY STEP

The first rounds start out just like the others, but we have a change starting from round 8 that will create the curve at the end of the tail.

Rounds 8–10: To make the curve in the tail, you're going to work half the round with half double crochets (to make larger stitches) and the other half with slip stitches (so as not to create too much thickness). Be careful not to tighten your slip stitches too much because you're going to need to do several rows of these and it will become much too difficult to insert your hook through very tight stitches.

Round 11: The three most important rounds for positioning the tail are complete, but you'll make one last round with half single crochets and half slip stitches to finish this section.

Now you can finish the tail like the other elements, making simple rounds of single crochets before starting your decreases. Remember to stuff as you work and to keep enough yarn at the end so you can sew.

SALLY SQUIRREL'S EARS, STEP BY STEP

There is nothing too special about the ears in and of themselves, except for the little tufts of "fur" added to the tip of each ear. Here's how to make them:

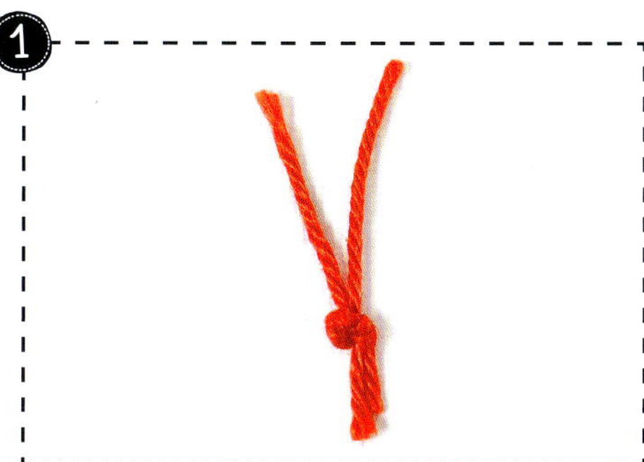

Cut two pieces of yarn about 2″ (5cm) long and knot them together.

Use your yarn needle to thread them (from the inside out) through the center of the magic ring (round 0 of the ears). Go until you reach the knot, which will prevent them from coming out.

Once the yarn is through, cut them to the desired length and unravel the strands to create the little tufts at the end of the ears.

SEWING

Placement is indicated on the previous page. As always, I recommend positioning everything with pins to help you hold the elements in place on the body. You don't have to do everything all at once, but I do recommend starting at the top of the body and working your way down. It's important to place the legs and tail at the same time to balance the amigurumi.

Take your time, play some music or set yourself some goals, whatever works best for you. This is a long step and one you may be tempted to put off, but your pride when the task is complete will be that much greater because of the time you put into it.

I learn about THE COMPLEX MAGIC RING AND INVISIBLE DECREASE

MATERIALS

- E-4 crochet hook (3.50mm)
- Fine/sport weight cotton yarn
- Scissors
- Stitch marker

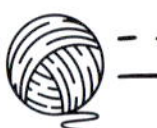

COMPLEX MAGIC RING

On Day 3 you learned how to make a "simple" magic ring, how to create a perfect circle in which you need to secure the yarn so it won't open back up. There is a technique for a perfect circle that can't reopen so you don't need to add the extra knot. This technique is a little more complex. Here are the steps:

1a

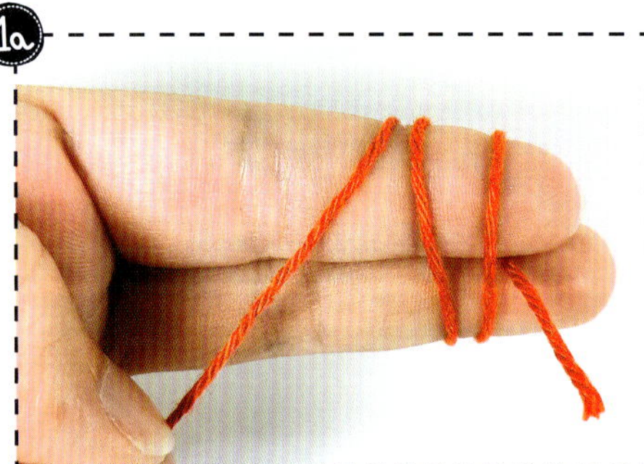

Wrap the yarn twice around your fingers from left to right. Hold the yarn between your fingers to maintain the right tension.

1b

Here is another view of how to hold the yarn.

2

Slip the hook under two strands to reach the last (the leftmost yarn).

3

Draw this yarn under the two you went under in Step 2, making a loop on your hook.

4

Yarn over (wrap the yarn around your hook).

5

Draw the yarn you've wrapped around your hook through the loop already on it.

6

You can now very carefully remove the ring from your fingers to continue working your way around.

Make sure not to pull on the yarn just like during the earlier lesson.

7

Insert your hook through the ring.

Note: Because the ring is made up of two strands of yarn, make sure you go under both. For now, the steps are the same as for Day 3.

8

Yarn over (wrap the yarn around your hook).

9

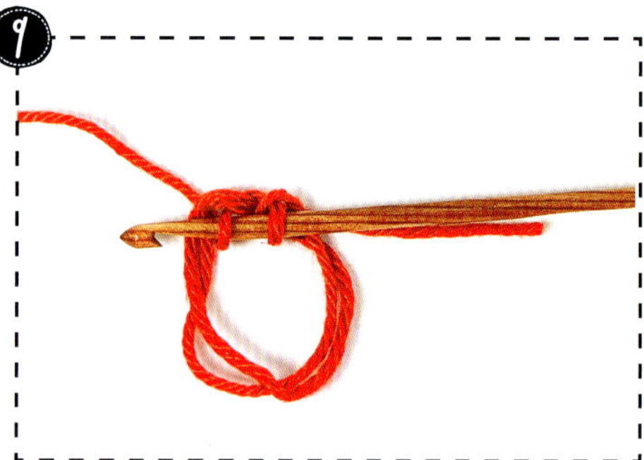

Draw the yarn you've wrapped around your hook through the ring.

10

Finish your stitch by yarning over again (wrap the yarn around your hook) before drawing the yarn through the two loops on your hook.

You have just made your first single crochet.

11

Make five more single crochets (for a total of six).

12

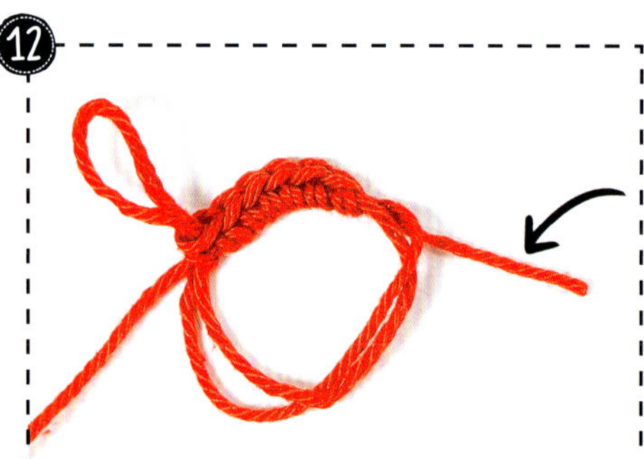

It's best to remove your hook for this last step, so widen the working loop so as not to lose it.

Now pull on the end of the yarn (indicated by an arrow).

13

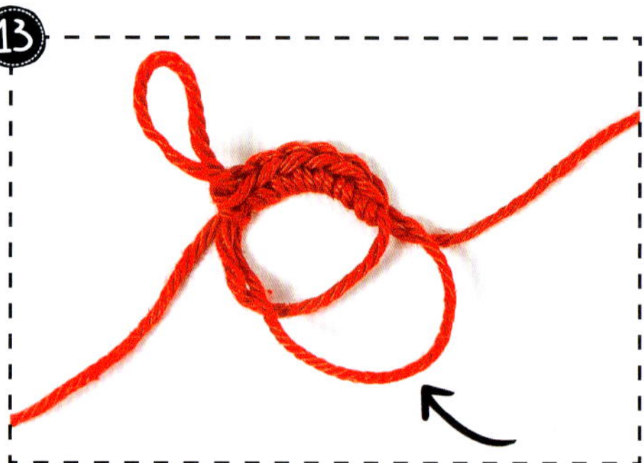

Pulling on the yarn will tighten one of the two loops that make up your ring.

Once you've figured out which one stays bigger (indicated by an arrow), pull on it.

14

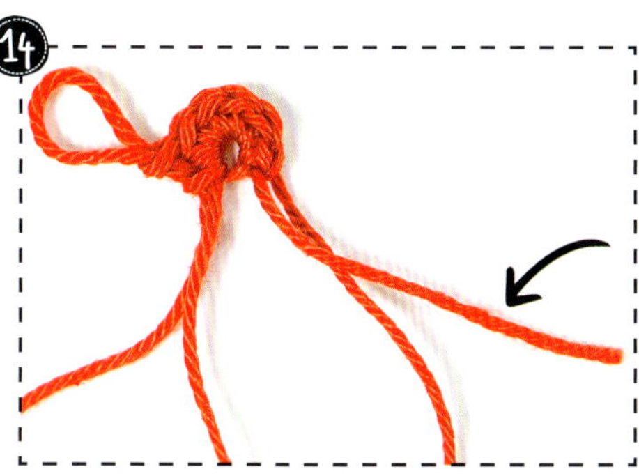

Once this loop is pulled as far as it can, your ring will be closed and you have only the yarn you've just pulled and the end of the yarn.

Once again pull on the end so that the other one shrinks until it disappears. It may get a little stuck, but don't be scared to pull harder.

15

Your circle is finished, it will not open back up, and you can now return your hook to the working loop to make the rest of your rounds.

INVISIBLE DECREASE

On Day 2 you learned how to decrease, and that technique is valuable for anything you make. However, there is another version that allows you to create less visible decreases on your amigurumi.

1

Chain 11 then make two rows of single crochets.

2

Insert your hook under the front loop of the next stitch.

3

Next insert your hook under the front loop of the following stitch.

You therefore have on your hook the original loop and both front loops of the next two stitches.

4

Yarn over (wrap the yarn around your hook).

5

Draw your yarn through the two front loops under which you inserted your hook in steps 2 and 3.

6

Yarn over (wrap the yarn around your hook).

7

Draw the yarn through the two loops on your hook. You have just made an invisible decrease.

Do the same thing along your row to create a total of 5 decreases.

8

Your work will gather because of the decreases, but you can see that they are visually different: Instead of leaning to one side, they stand up and create a V shape like single crochets, making them less discernible.

Note: This method only works for amigurumi because on a project worked flat (back and forth), taking just the front loops makes these decreases very noticeable on the reverse side.

day 14

I make TEDDY TREE

PART 1

The time has arrived to begin your third amigurumi: Teddy Tree. For this one, you will call upon your knowledge of front loop and back loop, as well as picots for the foliage. Teddy Tree is crocheted in one piece, you will just have to sew on the arms and crochet the foliage directly on waiting front loops. For this first part, you will make the body. The trunk, foliage, and arms will wait until tomorrow.

MATERIALS

- D-3 crochet hook (3.00mm)
- Fine/sport weight cotton yarn
  - Green ≈ 88 yards (80m)
  - Brown ≈ 22 yards (20m)
- Stuffing
- Yarn needle/scissors/pins
- 2 safety eyes, 1/4″ (6mm)
- Stitch marker

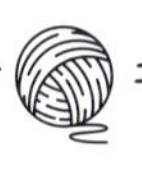

PATTERN Green

rnd 0 = Start with a magic ring
rnd 1 = 3 sc in the ring (3 st)
rnd 2 = 3 inc (6 st)
rnd 3 = *1 sc, inc* × 3 (9 st)
rnd 4 = 1 sc, inc, *2 sc, inc* × 2, 1 sc (12 st)
rnd 5 = *3 sc, inc* × 3 (15 st)
rnd 6 = 2 sc, inc, *4 sc, inc* × 2, 2 sc (18 st)
rnd 7 = [BL] *5 sc, inc* × 3 (21 st)
rnd 8 = 3 sc, inc, *6 sc, inc* × 2, 3 sc (24 st)
rnd 9 = *7 sc, inc* × 3 (27 st)
rnd 10 = 4 sc, inc, *8 sc, inc* × 2, 4 sc (30 st)
rnd 11 = [BL] *9 sc, inc* × 3 (33 st)
rnd 12 = 5 sc, inc, *10 sc, inc* × 2, 5 sc (36 st)
rnd 13 = *11 sc, inc* × 3 (39 st)
rnd 14 = 6 sc, inc, *12 sc, inc* × 2, 6 sc (42 st)
rnd 15 = [BL] *13 sc, inc* × 3 (45 st)
rnd 16 = 7 sc, inc, *14 sc, inc* × 2, 7 sc (48 st)
rnd 17 = *15 sc, inc* × 3 (51 st)
→ Place the safety eyes between rnds 17 and 18 (10 stitches in between)
rnd 18 = 8 sc, inc, *16 sc, inc* × 2, 8 sc (54 st)
rnd 19 = [BL] *17 sc, inc* × 3 (57 st)
rnd 20 = 9 sc, inc, *18 sc, inc* × 2, 9 sc (60 st)
rnd 21 = *19 sc, inc* × 3 (63 st)
rnd 22 = 10 sc, inc, *20 sc, inc* × 2, 10 sc (66 st)
rnd 23 = [BL] *21 sc, inc* × 3 (69 st)
rnd 24 = 11 sc, inc, *22 sc, inc* × 2, 11 sc (72 st)
rnd 25 = *23 sc, inc* × 3 (75 st)
rnd 26 = 12 sc, inc, *24 sc, inc* × 2, 12 sc (78 st)
rnd 27 = [BL] *11 sc, dec* × 6 (72 st)
rnd 28 = 5 sc, dec, *10 sc, dec* × 5, 5 sc (66 st)
rnd 29 = *9 sc, dec* × 6 (60 st)
rnd 30 = 4 sc, dec, *8 sc, dec* × 5, 4 sc (54 st)
→ For a flat base, see Tip

day 14

rnd 31 = *7 sc, dec* × 6 (48 st)
rnd 32 = 3 sc, dec, *6 sc, dec* × 5, 3 sc (42 st)
rnd 33 = *5 sc, dec* × 6 (36 st)
rnd 34 = 2 sc, dec, *4 sc, dec* × 5, 2 sc (30 st) → Remember to stuff!

Finish with a sl st, cut the yarn, and work it in.

You will stop here for today and come back to this spot tomorrow to make the trunk.

TEDDY TREE'S BODY, STEP BY STEP

You're going to start at the pointed end (the top) of Teddy Tree and make the base wider and wider. Increases are added very gradually, by threes, to create a cone.

Rounds 7, 11, 15, 19, 23, and 27: These are the rounds where you will work in the back loop only, leaving the front loop for tomorrow. Pay close attention to doing these rounds correctly.

TIP!

It's never easy to make a flat bottom on an amigurumi because of the stuffing, which always forms a little rounded. This step is not required, but if you want the bottom of Teddy Tree to be flat, you're going to have to "cheat" a little bit. Take a piece of rigid cardboard (or plastic) and place the largest round (round 26) of your amigurumi on top to trace the outline. Then cut the cardboard (or plastic), and don't forget to cut a hole in the middle (to help with stuffing). Once you've done this, continue on to rounds 27–30 before slipping this piece inside your work so that it stays in place. Once this is done, continue your rounds of decreases. It will be harder to get a good grip on your work because of this little engineering, so take your time.

See you tomorrow for the completion of Teddy Tree.

I make TEDDY TREE

PART 2

You've left Teddy Tree on hold at the 34th round, today you will complete this amigurumi.

MATÉRIEL

- D-3 crochet hook (3.00mm)
- Fine/sport weight cotton yarn
  - Green ≈ 88 yards (80m)
  - Brown ≈ 22 yards (20m)
- Stuffing
- Yarn needle/scissors/pins
- 2 safety eyes, 1/4″ (6mm)
- Stitch marker

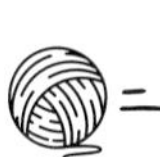

PATTERN **Trunk** / Brown

rnd 35 = (Brown) [FL] 30 sc
rnd 36–39 (4 rnds) = 30 sc
rnd 40 = 2 sc, inc, *4 sc, inc* × 5, 2 sc (36 st)
rnd 41 = [FL] *5 sc, inc, p* × 6 (42 st)

Finish with a sl st, cut the yarn, and work it in.

Return to the back loops you've left unworked in round 41 and do:

rnd 41 = [BL] 2 sc, dec, *4 sc, dec* × 5, 2 sc (30 st)
rnd 42 = *3 sc, dec* × 6 (24 st)—Remember to stuff!
rnd 43 = 1 sc, dec, *2 sc, dec* × 5, 1 sc (18 st)
rnd 44 = *1 sc, dec* × 6 (12 st)
rnd 45 = 6 dec (6 st)

Stuff firmly (while still maintaining a stable base. You can use the tip from Day 14 again if you choose). Cut the yarn and, using a yarn needle, work it through the 6 remaining stitches, tighten, and cut.

PATTERN **Foliage** / Green

To make the foliage, you will return to the front loops on the tree that you left unworked.

rnd 7 = [FL] *3 sc, p* × 6, 1 sl st, cut and work the yarn in (18 st)
rnd 11 = [FL] *3 sc, p* × 10, 1 sl st, cut and work the yarn in (30 st)
rnd 15 = [FL] *3 sc, p* × 14, 1 sl st, cut and work the yarn in (42 st)
rnd 19 = [FL] *3 sc, p* × 18, 1 sl st, cut and work the yarn in (54 st)
rnd 23 = [FL] *3 sc, p* × 22, 1 sl st, cut and work the yarn in (66 st)
rnd 27 = [FL] *3 sc, p* × 26, 1 sl st, cut and work the yarn in (78 st)

PATTERN **Arms / Make 2 /** Brown

rnd 0 = Start with a magic ring
rnd 1 = 6 sc in the ring (6 st)
rnd 2 = *1 sc, inc* × 3 (9 st)
rnd 3–6 (4 rnds) = 9 sc

Stuff loosely. Finish with a sl st and cut the yarn, keeping enough length to sew the arms on either side of the tree between rounds 23 and 26.

TEDDY TREE'S TRUNK, STEP BY STEP

Yesterday you stopped in the creation of Teddy Tree at round 34 in green. Now take up your brown yarn to continue your work by making the trunk.

Rounds 41: This round is worked twice: once in the front loops to create the roots, and once in the back loops to start the rounds of decreases to close Teddy Tree.

The tip from yesterday can be used again to achieve a flat base under your Teddy Tree's trunk. That's up to you. In either case, be careful when stuffing so the amigurumi remains stable.

TEDDY TREE'S FOLIAGE, STEP BY STEP

You are now going to return to the unworked front loops from yesterday (Day 14) on rounds 7, 11, 15, 19, 23, and 27. You will make picots and single crochets (not slip stitches this time, because you need to create some thickness) all around the body of the tree to create the foliage.

→ You should point Teddy Tree's top toward you as you work these 6 rounds, meaning you will work in the same direction in which you crocheted the original rounds.

Each slip stitch at the rounds' ends is crocheted in the first single crochet from the beginning (this allows you to close the round you've just done) before cutting the yarn and working it in. These six rounds will therefore be separate.

TEDDY TREE'S ARMS, STEP BY STEP

These are made the same way as Sally Squirrel's, though smaller. Stuff them loosely before sewing them on Teddy Tree's sides, using pins to help you.

And there you go! You have now created Teddy Tree, the first of your complex amigurumi!

I learn THE LOOP STITCH

Here's your first crochet stitch that is a little more complex: the loop stitch. This stitch will let you make hair, manes, fur, spines, or other features to give certain amigurumi their unique characteristics. Take your time to find the right yarn tension and the movements that work best for you.

MATERIALS

- E-4 crochet hook (3.50mm)
- Fine/sport weight cotton yarn
- Scissors
- Stitch marker

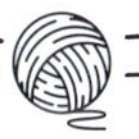

1

Make two rows of ten single crochets before starting your loop stitches (as usual).

2

Insert your hook into the first stitch of the previous row and use your index finger to extend the yarn.

3

Move your hook to the right of the extended yarn.

4

Go into your hand to grab the yarn and draw it (along with the yarn you went around before) through the stitch into which you inserted your hook in Step 2.

Note: Your index finger provides the gauge for your loop stitch.

5

You now have 3 loops on your hook: the starting loop, then the two you have just drawn through the stitch.

The loop for your loop stitch is still around your finger.

6

Yarn over (wrap the yarn around your hook).

7

Draw the yarn through the three loops on your hook.

8

Here is your first loop stitch:

On the front, you have a stitch that looks like an X-shaped single crochet because you did not yarn over to draw it through your stitch (see Day 7).

On the back, the loop comes out.

You will now make a second in the same way: Insert your hook through the next stitch, extending the yarn around your index finger.

Move your hook around on the right side of the yarn to grab the yarn deeper in your hand.

Draw both through the stitch into which you inserted your hook in Step 9.

So you don't have to hold your finger up, after drawing the yarns through in Step 11, you can remove the loop from your finger and hold it with your index finger on the back of the work while you finish the stitch.

This will give your finger a break.

Yarn over again (wrap the yarn around your hook).

Draw the yarn through the three loops on your hook.

Here you have two loop stitches viewed from the back of the work.

Repeat these steps all along the row.

Once your row is finished, you have a "flat" row on the front of your work (visually, with X-shaped stitches).

Meanwhile on the back of the work, the loops appear.

Note: It is possible to make loops on the front of a work, but the method for doing this does not hold together as well as the one presented here, so I don't recommend it for amigurumi (stitches that loosen = problems with stuffing).

We will see how to deal with any front side/back side issues during the next amigurumi (Days 17–18).

Make a row of single crochets.

Note: When you work in rows (back and forth), you have to do the loop stitches on every other row to have all the loops on the same side.

19

Then make a new row of loop stitches.

Here is the result. Depending on the tension in the yarn around your finger, your loops will vary in size. Don't let it bother you, it's impossible to make anything identical (and if they were identical, it wouldn't reflect nature!).

Don't hesitate to make a few more rows to really understand how it feels and to find the movements and tension that work best for you.

INCREASES AND DECREASES WITH THE LOOP STITCH

These are made the same way as increases and invisible decreases (Day 13) with single crochets.

INCREASING

20

Make a loop stitch in the first stitch of your row (indicated by a green arrow).

21a

Make a second loop stitch in the same spot, as you would for a single crochet increase.

21b

On the other side, you now have two loops coming from the same spot.

DECREASING

22

Insert your hook through the front loops of the first two stitches, as you would for an invisible decrease.

23

Now make your loop stitch as you normally would: Go around the right of the yarn to draw it and the yarn within your hand through the loops into which you inserted your hook in Step 22. Then yarn over and finish your stitch.

24a

You have completed your decrease: From two stitches (indicated by dots), you have a single stitch (indicated by an arrow).

24b

Here is the single loop you get from working these two stitches.

Now you have all you need to get started on Sheila Sheep tomorrow.

day 17

I make SHEILA SHEEP

PART 1

After a good day of learning and practicing the loop stitch, you will make your first amigurumi using this technique. Take your time, as always. Today you're going to make the body because it requires a lot of concentration. You will do all the little elements tomorrow, even though there are quite a few.

MATERIALS

- D-3 crochet hook (3.00mm)
- Fine/sport weight cotton yarn
  - Ecru ≈ 110 yards (100m)
  - Cream ≈ 55 yards (50m)
  - Black ≈ 3 yards (3m)
- Stuffing
- Yarn needle/scissors/pins
- 2 safety eyes, ¼" (6mm)
- Stitch marker

PATTERN **Body /** Cream and Ecru

rnd 0 = (Cream) Start with a magic ring
rnd 1 = 6 sc in the ring (6 st)
rnd 2 = 6 inc (12 st)
rnd 3 = *1 sc, inc* × 6 (18 st)
rnd 4 = 1 sc, inc, *2 sc, inc* × 5, 1 sc (24 st)
rnd 5 = *3 sc, inc* × 6 (30 st)
rnd 6 = 30 sc
rnd 7 = 2 sc, inc, *4 sc, inc* × 5, 2 sc (36 st)
rnd 8 = 36 sc
rnd 9 = *5 sc, inc* × 6 (42 st)
rnd 10–12 (3 rnds) = 42 sc
→ Place the eyes between rounds 9 and 10 with 7 stitches in between.

Finish with a sl st, cut the yarn and work it in. Turn the work over to now crochet with the wrong side facing you because the loop stitches produce a loop on the back (the "outside"), so it's necessary to turn your work over to have the right sides of the single crochets in cream paired with the loops in ecru.

rnd 13–25 (13 rnds) = (Ecru) 42 lp st
rnd 26 = *5 lp st, dec-lp* × 6 (36 st)
rnd 27 = 36 lp st → Remember to start stuffing.
rnd 28 = 2 lp st, dec-lp, *4 lp st, dec-lp* × 5, 2 lp st (30 st)
rnd 29 = *3 lp st, dec-lp* × 6 (24 st)

Turn the work so the outside is out! The last three rounds will be a little more difficult to keep the yarn in the right direction (so you will be moving your hook from the inside outward [see photo]).

rnd 30 = 1 lp st, dec-lp, *2 lp st, dec-lp* × 5, 1 lp st (18 st)
rnd 31 = *1 lp st, dec-lp* × 6 (12 st)
rnd 32 = 6 dec-lp (6 st)

Stuff firmly. Cut the yarn and, using a yarn needle, thread it through the last 6 stitches, tighten, and work it in.

SHEILA SHEEP'S BODY, STEP BY STEP

Rounds 0–1: Start with a magic circle in cream with 6 single crochets inside it. Remember to place your stitch marker so you don't lose the beginning of your round.

Rounds 2–12: These are the starting rounds of an amigurumi which you already know, having done the same for Sally Squirrel. Remember to place the safety eyes and fasten off as you learned on Day 3.

Rounds 13–29: After that, turn your work so you have the back toward you, also explained on Day 3. Because loop stitches create a loop on the back of the work, this change is necessary to have the right side of rounds 2–13 together with the loop side of these rounds.

→ Remember to change colors before embarking on your loop stitch rounds.

Rounds 30–32: Currently you have all your loops on the inside of the amigurumi's body, so it's time to get them on the right side. To do this, turn your work to get the outside out. Be careful not to pull on the yarn, do it gently and, once done, take the opportunity to stuff. The three last rounds will be the trickiest because you need to reorient yourself in your crocheting, taking your stitches from the inside toward the outside. Don't worry, you're almost done!

The last step will be to stuff firmly and then work in the yarn. There you are, the most complex part is behind you!

We'll be back tomorrow for all the little elements!

day 18

I make SHEILA SHEEP

PART 2

Today you will make all the little additions that make up Sheila Sheep. You have made amigurumi arms and legs a few times now, therefore they will not be explained so that we can focus more on the bonnet, tail, and ears.

MATERIALS

- D-3 crochet hook (3.00mm)
- Fine/sport weight cotton yarn
  - Ecru ≈ 110 yards (100m)
  - Cream ≈ 55 yards (50m)
  - Black ≈ 3 yards (3m)
- Stuffing
- Yarn needle/scissors/pins
- 2 safety eyes, 1/4″ (6mm)
- Stitch marker

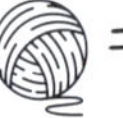

PATTERN **Arms / Make 2 /** Cream

rnd 0 = Start with a magic ring
rnd 1 = 6 sc in the ring (6 st)
rnd 2 = *1 sc, inc* × 3 (9 st)
rnd 3–8 (6 rnds) = 9 sc → Remember to start stuffing.
rnd 9 = *1 sc, dec* × 3 (6 st)

Stuff loosely. Cut the yarn and, using a yarn needle, run it through the 6 remaining stitches and tighten. Don't forget to keep enough length for sewing (see remaining steps).

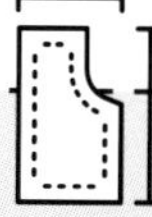

PATTERN **Legs / Make 2 /** Cream

rnd 0 = Start with a magic ring
rnd 1 = 6 sc in the ring (6 st)
rnd 2 = 6 inc (12 st)
rnd 3 = [BL] 12 sc
rnd 4 = 12 st
rnd 5 = 3 sc, 3 dec, 3 sc (9 st)
rnd 6–8 (3 rnds) = 9 sc
rnd 9 = *1 sc, dec* × 3 (6 st)

Stuff firmly. Cut the yarn and, using a yarn needle, run it through the 6 remaining stitches and tighten. Don't forget to keep enough length for sewing (see remaining steps).

PATTERN **Bonnet** / Ecru

rnd 0 = Start with a magic ring
rnd 1 = 6 sc in the ring (6 st)–(Or 6 lp st if you want to challenge yourself)
rnd 2 = 6 inc-lp (12 st)
rnd 3 = *1 lp st, inc-lp* × 6 (18 st)
rnd 4 = 1 lp st, inc-lp, *2 lp st, inc-lp* × 5, 1 lp st (24 st)
rnd 5 = *3 lp st, inc-lp* × 6 (30 st)
rnd 6 = 2 lp st, inc-lp, *4 lp st, inc-lp* × 5, 2 lp st (36 st)
rnd 7–9 (3 rnds) = 36 lp st

Finish with a sl st, cut the yarn. Don't forget to leave enough length for sewing (see remaining steps).

PATTERN **Ears / Make 2 of each color /** Cream and Ecru

rnd 0 = Start with a magic ring
rnd 1 = 6 sc in the ring (6 st)
rnd 2 = 6 inc (12 st)
rnd 3 = *1 sc, inc* × 6 (18 st)
rnd 4 = 1 sc, inc, *2 sc, inc* × 5, 1 sc (24 st)

Finish with a sl st, cut the yarn and work it in. Make the two ecru circles first. Next make a cream circle (without cutting the yarn) and place it against an ecru circle with wrong sides together (the right side of the cream circle facing you), then crochet them together with the cream yarn doing the fifth round (see below), inserting the hook through both layers at the same time (cream and ecru) (see Day 4).

rnd 5 = *3 sc, inc* × 6 (30 st)

Fold the ear in half and sew 4 stitches together with a needle (sewing through both layers) to create a fold. Finish with a sl st, cut the yarn. Don't forget to leave enough length for sewing (see remaining steps). Make a second ear the same way.

PATTERN **Tail** / Cream

rnd 0 = Start with a magic ring
rnd 1= 6 sc in the ring (6 st)–(Or 6 lp st if you want to challenge yourself)
rnd 2 = 6 inc-lp (12 st)
rnd 3–4 (2 rnds) = 12 lp st

Stuff firmly, finish with a sl st, and cut the yarn. Don't forget to keep enough length for sewing (see remaining steps).

REMAINING STEPS

All of this is provided as a guide, you can do however you please.

Bonnet/Head Assembly

The bonnet is placed on the head, slightly back so you can sew the back edge of the bonnet to the first round of loop stitches (round 13 on the back of the body). On the front, it reaches to one round above the eyes.

Ears/Bonnet Assembly

The ears are placed starting at round 6 of the bonnet, on either side of the head, drooping down.

Arms/Body Assembly

The arms are placed between rounds 16 and 18, on either side of the body.

Legs/Body Assembly

The legs are positioned from round 30 to round 26 in a V. Pay attention to Sheila Sheep's stability (place the tail with pins to be sure everything is balanced).

Tail/Body Assembly

The tail is placed from round 29 to round 26.

THE BONNET AND THE TAIL, STEP BY STEP

Rounds 0–1: It would look better to make loop stitches in your magic ring; however, if this is still too difficult for you, it's fine to simply make a row of single crochets in order to maintain your serenity. The loops from all the other rows will hide the single crochets.

The other rounds: Next take your time making loop stitch increases (Day 16) and don't forget to turn your work over once you've finished so that the loops are on the outside.

THE EARS, STEP BY STEP

These are made up of two circles, one in cream and the other in ecru, which you will then put together. Start with the two ecru circles before making your first cream circle. You will then make the fifth round in cream, crocheting in both layers (one cream and one ecru, wrong sides together) as you did on Day 4. Once this is done, make a second cream circle and crochet it to the second ecru circle.

SEWING

Get out your pins, it's time to sew (and it won't be very easy given the loops). As I've said before, you can certainly decide to place these elements elsewhere (especially the ears) if you prefer.

First of all, I recommend starting with the bonnet and ears:

The bonnet is placed on the head, slightly back so you can sew the back edge of the bonnet to the beginning of the loop stitch rounds (round 13 on the back of the body). On the front, the bonnet comes to one round above the eyes. Sew these seams before making a few little stitches for the snout.

For the ears, take your needle, fold the ear, and sew 4 stitches together so the ear stays creased. Once this is done, place them at round 6 of the bonnet, on either side of the head, hanging downward.

The rest of the elements are placed similarly to Sally Squirrel. Make sure to hold the loops aside so they don't get caught up in your sewing, that will be the most complicated part of this step. Remember to position the legs and tail at the same time to make sure Sheila Sheep is balanced.

And there's your finished amigurumi!

day 19

I learn THE POPCORN STITCH

Bobbles (also called the popcorn stitch) are one of the more complex techniques because they take time and a lot of yarn. However, they allow you to give texture to your work and, with a little practice, you'll be able to make them without even thinking about it.

Note: You will be doing the first steps of making a double crochet. If you're unsure, don't hesitate to make some double crochets for practice before moving on (see Day 10).

MATERIALS

- E-4 crochet hook (3.50mm)
- Fine/sport weight cotton yarn
- Scissors
- Stitch marker

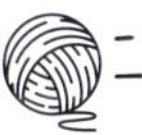

1

Chain 11 then make two rows of 10 single crochets (as usual) before starting your bobbles.

2

Yarn over (wrap the yarn around your hook).

3

Insert your hook into the first stitch of the previous row.

4

Yarn over (wrap the yarn around your hook).

5

Draw the yarn through the stitch into which you inserted your hook in Step 3.

6

Yarn over (wrap the yarn around your hook).

7

Draw the yarn through the two leftmost loops on your hook.

Here is where you stop the double crochet steps (you will not do the last step), so you have two loops on your hook.

8

Yarn over before again inserting your hook into the same stitch from Step 3 and then repeat Steps 4–7.

You now have three loops on your hook.

9

Yarn over before again inserting your hook into the same stitch from Step 3 and then repeat Steps 4–7.

You now have four loops on your hook.

10

Yarn over before again inserting your hook into the same stitch from Step 3 and then repeat Steps 4–7.

You now have five loops on your hook.

11

Yarn over (wrap the yarn around your hook).

12

Draw the yarn through all five loops on your hook.

13

Bobbles have a tendency to come out on the back side of the work, so don't hesitate to reshape it by pressing it toward you before doing the next step.

14

Next insert your hook into the next stitch and make a single crochet.

Note: If the bobble still comes out the back, don't hesitate to push it forward with the end of your hook so that it stays in the right place.

15

Here is the result. The single crochet is there to make the bobble stick out.

16

Repeat Steps 2–10 in the next stitch to get five loops on your hook.

17

Yarn over, draw the yarn through your five loops to make your second bobble.

Push it into position (toward the front) and make a single crochet.

18

Finish your row of bobbles, alternating between a bobble and a single crochet.

19

Make a row of single crochets.

I recommend always putting a row of single crochets between two rows of bobbles to tighten up your work (as ever, with the intention of keeping the stuffing inside the amigurumi).

20

Make a new row of bobbles, always alternating bobbles and single crochets.

day 20

I make BRADLEY BEAR

PART 1

And so Bradley Bear comes to be, made entirely of bobbles to add some texture. As with Sheila Sheep, today you will focus only on the body, because that's what will take the most time. Relax, and here we go!

MATERIALS

- D-3 crochet hook (3.00mm)
- Fine/sport weight cotton yarn
  - Brown ≈ 130 yards (120m)
  - Black ≈ 3 yards (3m)
- Stuffing
- Yarn needle/scissors/pins
- 2 safety eyes, 1/4″ (6mm)
- Stitch marker

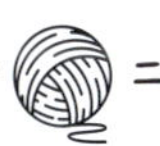

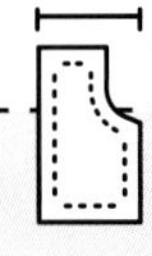

PATTERN Body / Brown

rnd 0 = Start with a magic ring
rnd 1 = 6 sc in the ring (6 st)
rnd 2 = {1 sc, 1 bo} × 6 (12 st)
rnd 3 = 12 inc (24 st)
rnd 4 = *1 bo, 1 sc* × 12 (24 st)
rnd 5 = *3 sc, inc* × 6 (30 st)
rnd 6 = *1 bo, 1 sc* × 15 (30 st)
rnd 7 = 2 sc, inc, *4 sc, inc* × 5, 2 sc (36 st)
rnd 8 = *1 bo, 1 sc* × 18 (36 st)
rnd 9 = *5 sc, inc* × 6 (42 st)
rnd 10 = *1 bo, 1 sc* × 21 (42 st)
→ Place the eyes between rounds 9 and 10 with 7 stitches in between.
rnd 11 = 42 sc
rnd 12 = *1 bo, 1 sc* × 21 (42 st)
rnd 13 = 42 sc
rnd 14 = *1 bo, 1 sc* × 21 (42 st)
rnd 15 = 42 sc
rnd 16 = *1 bo, 1 sc* × 21 (42 st)
rnd 17 = 42 sc
rnd 18 = *1 bo, 1 sc* × 21 (42 st)
rnd 19 = 42 sc
rnd 20 = *1 bo, 1 sc* × 21 (42 st)
rnd 21 = 42 sc
rnd 22 = *1 bo, 1 sc* × 21 (42 st)
rnd 23 = 42 sc
rnd 24 = *1 bo, 1 sc* × 21 (42 st) → Remember to start stuffing.
rnd 25 = *5 sc, dec* × 6 (36 st)
rnd 26 = *1 bo, 1 sc* × 18 (36 st)
rnd 27 = 2 sc, dec, *4 sc, dec* × 5, 2 sc (30 st)
rnd 28 = *1 bo, 1 sc, 1 bo, dec* × 6 (24 st)
rnd 29 = 1 sc, dec, *2 sc, dec* × 5, 1 sc (18 st)
rnd 30 = *1 bo, dec* × 6 (12 st)
rnd 31 = 6 dec (6 st)

Stuff firmly. Cut the yarn and, using a yarn needle, run it through the 6 remaining stitches, tighten, and work the yarn in.

day 20

BRADLEY BEAR'S BODY, STEP BY STEP

Rounds 0–1: Start with a magic ring in brown with 6 single crochets in it. Remember to place your stitch marker so you don't lose the beginning of your round.

Round 2: This round is a little different because to increase to 12 stitches, you will make one bobble and one single crochet in each stitch (instead of two single crochets in each stitch). Take your time, this isn't easy.

As explained on Day 19, you are going to alternate one round with bobbles and one round of single crochets for the whole body. This will allow the stitches to tighten because they will often be looser on rows of bobbles.

→ Remember to place the safety eyes and stuff as you work. If you find it too difficult to make bobbles on round 30, just do single crochets instead. It's the bottom of Bradley Bear so it's not a big deal.

You're all done with the bobbles, take it easy with the little elements tomorrow.

I make BRADLEY BEAR
PART 2

Here we are on the last day of this book. I hope you've enjoyed learning about crocheting amigurumi, and that you want to continue populating your little amigurumi world! Today you will make the final pieces of Bradley Bear and assemble them. Nothing complex here, as you've already made arms and legs on several occasions. The snout, tail, and ears are made the same way, so there's no surprises there. Only the sewing may be a little complicated, as always.

MATERIALS

- D-3 crochet hook (3.00mm)
- Fine/sport weight cotton yarn
  - Brown ≈ 130 yards (120m)
  - Black ≈ 3 yards (3m)
- Stuffing
- Yarn needle/scissors/pins
- 2 safety eyes, 1/4" (6mm)
- Stitch marker

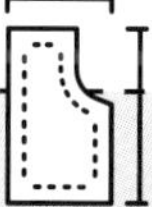

PATTERN **Ears / Make 2 /** Brown

rnd 0 = Start with a magic ring
rnd 1 = 6 sc in the ring (6 st)
rnd 2 = 6 inc (12 st)
rnd 3 = *1 sc, inc* × 6 (18 st)
rnd 4 = 1 sc, inc, *2 sc, inc* × 5, 1 sc (24 st)
rnd 5–6 (2 rnds) = 24 sc

Finish with a sl st, cut the yarn. Don't forget to leave enough length for sewing (see remaining steps).

PATTERN **Snout** / Brown

rnd 0 = Start with a magic ring
rnd 1 = 6 sc in the ring (6 st)
rnd 2 = 6 inc (12 st)
rnd 3 = *1 sc, inc* × 6 (18 st)
rnd 4 = 18 sc
rnd 5 = 1 sc, inc, *2 sc, inc* × 5, 1 sc (24 st)

Stuff firmly, finish with a sl st, and cut the yarn. Don't forget to leave enough length for sewing (see remaining steps).

PATTERN **Arms / Make 2** / Brown

rnd 0 = Start with a magic ring
rnd 1 = 6 sc in the ring (6 st)
rnd 2 = *1 sc, inc* × 3 (9 st)
rnd 3–8 (6 rnds) = 9 sc
rnd 9 = *1 sc, dec* × 3 (6 st)

Stuff loosely. Cut the yarn and, using a yarn needle, work it through the 6 remaining stitches and tighten. Don't forget to leave enough length for sewing (see remaining steps).

PATTERN **Tail** / Brown

rnd 0 = Start with a magic ring
rnd 1 = 6 sc in the ring (6 st)
rnd 2 = 6 inc (12 st)
rnd 3–4 (2 rnds) = 12 sc

Stuff firmly, finish with a sl st, and cut the yarn. Don't forget to leave enough length for sewing (see remaining steps).

PATTERN **Legs / Make 2** / Brown

rnd 0 = Start with a magic ring
rnd 1 = 6 sc in the ring (6 st)
rnd 2 = 6 inc (12 st)
rnd 3 = [BL] 12 sc
rnd 4 = 12 st
rnd 5 = 3 sc, 3 dec, 3 sc (9 st)
rnd 6–8 (3 rnds) = 9 sc
rnd 9 = *1 sc, dec* × 3 (6 st)

Stuff firmly, finish with a sl st, and cut the yarn. Don't forget to leave enough length for sewing (see remaining steps).

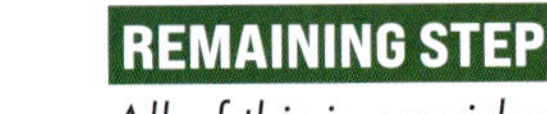

REMAINING STEPS

All of this is provided as a guide, you can do however you please.

Ears/Body Assembly

Curve (slightly fold) the ears to make them cupped. Then place them between rounds 4 and 9 on either side of the head.

Snout/Body Assembly

The top of the snout is placed level with the eyes. Center it. Use black yarn to embroider the nose (see photo).

Arms/Body Assembly

The arms are placed between rounds 15 and 17 on either side of the body.

Legs/Body Assembly

The legs are positioned from round 29 to round 26 in a V shape. Pay attention to Bradley Bear's stability (place the tail with pins to be sure everything is balanced).

Tail/Body Assembly

The tail is placed from 26 to round 29.

BRADLEY BEAR'S APPENDAGES, STEP BY STEP

Take your time, there is nothing too complex. This is an easy day after bobble-filled Day 20.

SEWING

The ears are the most difficult to attach. Without folding them completely (unlike Sheila Sheep), you need to curve the ears to place them correctly. Don't hesitate to use as many pins as you need, it costs nothing and it helps.

The snout is placed level with the eyes. Don't forget to stitch the nose in black on the snout. To do this, just sew with yarn, always starting from the center of the ring outward. Make it as wide as you like.

The arms, legs, and tail are placed like on the other amigurumi. Don't forget to position the tail and legs at the same time to make sure Bradley Bear is balanced.

And there you have it, you've finished your 21 days and learned to crochet amigurumi! Come back tomorrow for one last big amigurumi.

bonus

I make MUSHROOM HOUSE

And here's a bonus to your 21 days, a larger amigurumi to watch over all the amigurumi you've already made. Here you will find the pattern (without explanations this time) and one last lesson. Happy crocheting!

MATERIALS

- D-3 crochet hook (3.00mm)
- Fine/sport weight cotton yarn
  - White ≈ 130 yards (120m)
  - Cream ≈ 71 yards (65m)
  - Brown ≈ 88 yards (80m)
  - Red ≈ 110 yards (100m)
  - Yellow ≈ 27 yards (25m)
  - Orange ≈ 11 yards (10m)
  - Green ≈ 11 yards (10m)
- Stuffing
- Yarn needle/scissors
- Stitch marker

PATTERN **Stalk and gills /**
Brown, Cream, and White

rnd 0 = (Brown) Start with a magic ring
rnd 1 = 6 sc in the ring (6 st)
rnd 2 = 6 inc (12 st)
rnd 3 = *1 sc, inc* × 6 (18 st)
rnd 4 = 1 sc, inc, *2 sc, inc* × 5, 1 sc (24 st)
rnd 5 = *3 sc, inc* × 6 (30 st)
rnd 6 = 2 sc, inc, *4 sc, inc* × 5, 2 sc (36 st)
rnd 7 = *5 sc, inc* × 6 (42 st)
rnd 8 = 3 sc, inc, *6 sc, inc* × 5, 3 sc (48 st)
rnd 9 = *7 sc, inc* × 6 (54 st)
rnd 10 = 4 sc, inc, *8 sc, inc* × 5, 4 sc (60 st)
rnd 11 = *9 sc, inc* × 6 (66 st)
rnd 12 = 5 sc, inc, *10 sc, inc* × 5, 5 sc (72 st)
rnd 13 = *11 sc, inc* × 6 (78 st)
rnd 14 = 6 sc, inc, *12 sc, inc* × 5, 6 sc (84 st)
rnd 15 = *13 sc, inc* × 6 (90 st)
rnd 16 = 7 sc, inc, *14 sc, inc* × 5, 7 sc (96 st)
rnd 17 = *15 sc, inc* × 6 (102 st)
rnd 18 = 8 sc, inc, *16 sc, inc* × 5, 8 sc (108 st)
rnd 19–20 (2 rnds) = 108 sc
rnd 21 = (Brown) 2 sc, *(Cream) 2 sc, (Brown) 4 sc* × 17, (Cream) 2 sc, (Brown) 2 sc (108 st)
rnd 22 = (Brown) 1 sc, *(Cream) 4 sc, (Brown) 2 sc* × 17, (Cream) 5 sc (108 st)
rnd 23–24 (2 rnds) = (Cream) 108 sc
rnd 25 = (Cream) 2 sc, *(White) 2 sc, (Cream) 4 sc* × 17, (White) 2 sc, (Cream) 2 sc (108 st)
rnd 26 = (Cream) 1 sc, *(White) 4 sc, (Cream) 2 sc* × 17, (White) 5 sc (108 st)
rnd 27–29 (3 rnds) = (White) 108 sc
rnd 30 = 8 sc, dec, *16 sc, dec* × 5, 8 sc (102 st)
rnd 31–33 (3 rnds) = 102 sc

rnd 34 = *15 sc, dec* × 6 (96 st)
rnd 35–37 (3 rnds) = 96 sc
rnd 38 = 7 sc, dec, *14 sc, dec* × 5, 7 sc (90 st)
rnd 39–41 (3 rnds) = 90 sc
rnd 42 = *13 sc, dec* × 6 (84 st)
rnd 4–45 (3 rnds) = 84 sc
rnd 46 = 6 sc, dec, *12 sc, dec* × 5, 6 sc (78 st)
rnd 47–49 (3 rnds) = 78 sc
rnd 50 = *11 sc, dec* × 6 (72 st)
rnd 51–55 (5 rnds) = 72 sc
rnd 56 = [FL] (Cream) *11 sc, inc* × 6 (78 st)
rnd 57 = 6 sc, inc, *12 sc, inc* × 5, 6 sc (84 st)
rnd 58 = *13 sc, inc* × 6 (90 st)
rnd 59 = 7 sc, inc, *14 sc, inc* × 5, 7 sc (96 st)
rnd 60 = *15 sc, inc* × 6 (102 st)
rnd 61 = 8 sc, inc, *16 sc, inc* × 5, 8 sc (108 st)
rnd 62 = *17 sc, inc* × 6 (114 st)
rnd 63 = 9 sc, inc, *18 sc, inc* × 5, 9 sc (120 st)
rnd 64 = *19 sc, inc* × 6 (126 st)
rnd 65 = 10 sc, inc, *20 sc, inc* × 5, 10 sc (132 st)
rnd 66 = *21 sc, inc* × 6 (138 st)
rnd 67 = 11 sc, inc, *22 sc, inc* × 5, 11 sc (144 st)

Finish with a sl st, cut the yarn and work it in.

Do the green embroidery (lesson at the end of the pattern) before stuffing, because you will need to have access to the inside of the body to do so. Feel free to rely on the photos to see where to put it, because the door will need space as well. Then stuff Mushroom House's stalk firmly.

PATTERN Cap / Red

rnd 0 = Start with a magic ring
rnd 1 = 6 sc in the ring (6 st)
rnd 2 = 6 inc (12 st)
rnd 3 = *1 sc, inc* × 6 (18 st)
rnd 4 = 1 sc, inc, *2 sc, inc* × 5, 1 sc (24 st)
rnd 5 = *3 sc, inc* × 6 (30 st)
rnd 6 = 2 sc, inc, *4 sc, inc* × 5, 2 sc (36 st)
rnd 7 = *5 sc, inc* × 6 (42 st)
rnd 8 = 3 sc, inc, *6 sc, inc* × 5, 3 sc (48 st)
rnd 9 = *7 sc, inc* × 6 (54 st)
rnd 10 = 4 sc, inc, *8 sc, inc* × 5, 4 sc (60 st)
rnd 11 = *9 sc, inc* × 6 (66 st)
rnd 12 = 5 sc, inc, *10 sc, inc* × 5, 5 sc (72 st)
rnd 13 = *11 sc, inc* × 6 (78 st)
rnd 14 = 6 sc, inc, *12 sc, inc* × 5, 6 sc (84 st)
rnd 15 = *13 sc, inc* × 6 (90 st)
rnd 16 = 7 sc, inc, *14 sc, inc* × 5, 7 sc (96 st)
rnd 17 = *15 sc, inc* × 6 (102 st)
rnd 18 = 8 sc, inc, *16 sc, inc* × 5, 8 sc (108 st)
rnd 19 = *17 sc, inc* × 6 (114 st)
rnd 20 = 9 sc, inc, *18 sc, inc* × 5, 9 sc (120 st)
rnd 21 = *19 sc, inc* × 6 (126 st)
rnd 22 = 10 sc, inc, *20 sc, inc* × 5, 10 sc (132 st)
rnd 23 = *21 sc, inc* × 6 (138 st)
rnd 24 = 11 sc, inc, *22 sc, inc* × 5, 11 sc (144 st)
rnd 25–28 (4 rnds) = 144 sc

Round 29 of the cap will let you connect it to the gills. To do this, insert your hook through a stitch on the cap (round 28) and the back loop of one on the gills (round 67). The cap should be toward you, with the gills behind the cap. In this way, make a new round of 144 single crochets.

Make a pillow of stuffing a good half-inch (or centimeter) thick to give volume to the cap without overstuffing it, which would prevent it from "drooping" like a mushroom.

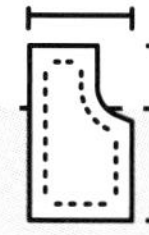

PATTERN **Door** / Brown

r 0 = Chain 23, turn
r 1–22 (22 rows) = 22 sc, ch 1, turn (22 st)
r 23 = dec, 18 sc, dec, ch 1, turn (20 st)
r 24 = dec, 16 sc, dec, ch 1, turn (18 st)
r 25 = dec, 14 sc, dec, ch 1, turn (16 st)
r 26 = dec, 12 sc, dec, ch 1, turn (14 st)
r 27 = dec, 10 sc, dec (12 st)

Cut the yarn, leaving enough length for sewing (at least 12″ or 30cm), then draw the yarn through the loop on your hook.

To finish, make a round of single crochets in brown to give the door neat edges and then add—if desired—an embroidered border in cream (lesson at the end of the pattern).

PATTERN **Doorknob** / Yellow

rnd 0 = Start with a magic ring
rnd 1 = 6 sc in the ring (6 st)
rnd 2 = 6 inc (12 st)

Finish with a sl st and cut the yarn. Don't forget to leave enough length for sewing (see remaining steps).

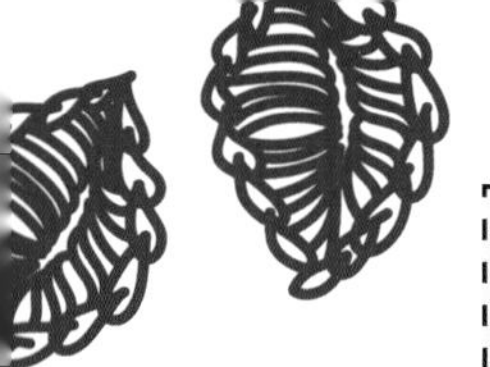
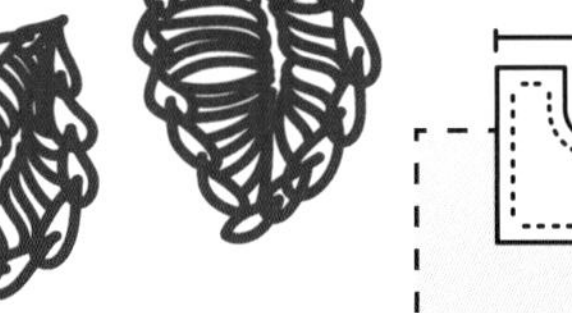

PATTERN **Spots** / White and Yellow

TWO LARGE (ONE WHITE AND ONE YELLOW)

rnd 0 = Start with a magic ring
rnd 1 = 6 sc in the ring (6 st)
rnd 2 = 6 inc (12 st)
rnd 3 = *1 sc, inc* × 6 (18 st)
rnd 4 = 1 sc, inc, *2 sc, inc* × 5, 1 sc (24 st)
rnd 5 = *3 sc, inc* × 6 (30 st)
rnd 6 = 2 sc, inc, *4 sc, inc* × 5, 2 sc (36 st)

Finish with a sl st and cut the yarn. Don't forget to leave enough length for sewing (see remaining steps).

THREE MEDIUM (TWO WHITE AND ONE YELLOW)

rnd 0 = Start with a magic ring
rnd 1 = 6 sc in the ring (6 st)
rnd 2 = 6 inc (12 st)
rnd 3 = *1 sc, inc* × 6 (18 st)
rnd 4 = 1 sc, inc, *2 sc, inc* × 5, 1 sc (24 st)
rnd 5 = *3 sc, inc* × 6 (30 st)

Finish with a sl st and cut the yarn. Don't forget to leave enough length for sewing (see remaining steps).

THREE SMALL (ONE WHITE AND TWO YELLOW)

rnd 0 = Start with a magic ring
rnd 1 = 6 sc in the ring (6 st)
rnd 2 = 6 inc (12 st)
rnd 3 = *1 sc, inc* × 6 (18 st)
rnd 4 = 1 sc, inc, *2 sc, inc* × 5, 1 sc (24 st)

Finish with a sl st and cut the yarn. Don't forget to leave enough length for sewing (see remaining steps).

TWO TINY (ONE WHITE AND ONE YELLOW)

rnd 0 = Start with a magic ring
rnd 1 = 6 sc in the ring (6 st)
rnd 2 = 6 inc (12 st)

Finish with a sl st and cut the yarn. Don't forget to leave enough length for sewing (see remaining steps).

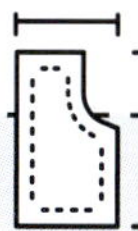

PATTERN Leaves / Yellow, Green, and Orange

These colors are one possible option, you can of course use whichever colors you please. You need to make a total of 12 leaves. On the model, there are 4 yellow, 4 green, and 4 orange.

rnd 0 = Chain 7 and turn
rnd 1 = Start in the second stitch from your hook (because you will be making half double crochets) and crochet: 3 hdc, 2 sc, {1 sc, p, 1 sc} (in the last stitch of your chain)—Don't turn but continue on the other side of the chain (starting with an oval)—2 sc, 3 hdc, ch 2

Finish with one sl st and cut the yarn. Don't forget to leave enough length for sewing (see remaining steps).

REMAINING STEPS

All of this is provided as a guide, you can do however you please.

Doorknob/House/Mushroom Assembly

Sew the doorknob to the door before sewing the door to the house, starting at round 19.

Spots/Cap Assembly

Scatter the spots on the cap however you like before sewing them on one by one.

Leaves/Stem Assembly (on the stalk)

Sew the leaves to the stems you've embroidered. Either at the end or somewhere along the stems, however you like. Have fun, this is your Mushroom House!

CROCHET EMBROIDERY

One last lesson for this bonus day. This is just so you can make any little detail you like on your amigurumi: crochet embroidery. This is done by making slip stitches with the work sandwiched in between.

1

Insert your hook where you want to start embroidering. Then make a slip knot on your hook.

2

Draw the loop of the knot through your work.

Note: Your yarn is now behind the work.

3

Insert your hook in the next hole (you have a "hole" between each stitch, that's where you need to insert your hook).

4

Hook the yarn.

5

Draw the yarn through your work.

6

Next draw the yarn through the first loop on your hook (the one on the right).

You have embroidered your first slip stitch.

Insert your hook in the next hole.

Hook the yarn and draw it through the work.

Next draw it through the first loop on your hook.

Here's the second slip stitch. Follow these steps to continue along your work.

Here is what you'll have when your line is finished.

Note: You've just made a straight line, but you can certainly make curves by inserting your hook through holes on the diagonal. Go ahead and test out this technique on your practice squares from earlier days.

CREATIVE
SPARK
ONLINE LEARNING

Ball